14

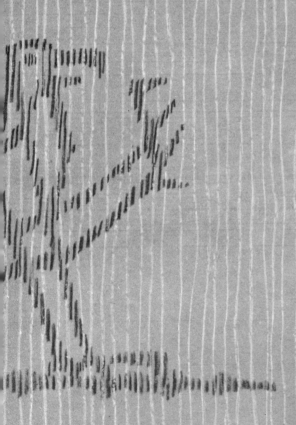

SPECIAL CONSULTANTS

THE GOLDEN TREASURY OF
KNOWLEDGE

VOLUME
14

OF SIXTEEN VOLUMES CONTAINING 420 BASIC
ARTICLES WITH 2500 ILLUSTRATIONS AND MAPS

Margaret Bevans
EDITOR-IN-CHIEF

Joanna Aldendorff
EDITORIAL CONSULTANT

Clifford Junceau
PROJECT CONSULTANT

Tom Torre Bevans
DIRECTOR

EDITORIAL STAFF

Renée Algrant · Doris Ballard · Richard Keigwin
I. W. Klein · Morgan Larkin · Henry Mins
Carol Z. Rothkopf · Peter Share

PRODUCTION STAFF

Rosalie Barrow · Frank Bologna · Ken Braren
Rosemary Gutwillig · Alan M. Heicklen
Yvonne Charles Johnson · Harris Lewine · Alice Lupo
Peter Marks · Tomaso Puliofito · Bruce Ross · Loretta Trezzo

COVER BY Ned Seidler

GOLDEN PRESS · NEW YORK

About VOLUME 14 and how it relates to other volumes

In this volume you will visit a famous London theater, discover remains of prehistoric men, and learn what makes birds fly. You will meet a famous painter and visit some beautiful ancient temples.

Any of the articles may interest you in other aspects of a subject. You can follow up your curiosity by consulting the index in Volume 16 under the name of the particular topic.

THE INTOLERABLE ACTS that led to the American Revolution may interest you in some Revolutionary people such as THOMAS JEFFERSON and BENJAMIN FRANKLIN. BIRDS may make you want to learn more about BIRDS' NESTS and MIGRATION OF BIRDS. THE AGE OF THE EARTH may interest you in GEOLOGY or THE PLANET EARTH in other volumes. COTTON may lead you to TEXTILE FIBERS or WOOL, and MEDIEVAL SEIGE WEAPONS may make you curious about the GROWTH OF WEAPONS.

It is fun and exciting to increase your knowledge of subjects that interest you. And in *The Golden Treasury of Knowledge* you will find a wide range of fascinating information for every interest.

© 1958, 1959, 1960 by Fratelli Fabbri Editori, Milan, Italy and published by special arrangement with them.
Copyright © 1961 by Golden Press, Inc. Designed by Bevans, Marks & Barrow, Inc. Printed in the U.S.A. by Western Printing and Lithographing Company.
Published by Golden Press, Inc., Rockefeller Center, New York 20, New York. Library of Congress Catalog Card Number: 61-10594.

CON

TENTS

See page 1237 for a time chart which will show how periods of history relate to one another and at what time many of the events in these articles took place.

An actor known as "the chorus" announced the coming action before the start of the play.

The Shakespearean Theater

In Elizabethan England when a flag flew from the top of the Globe Theater in London, it meant that a play would be performed there that day. The Globe was a roofless, wooden building near the south bank of the Thames River. It was three stories high and eight-sided. On seeing the signal flag, people hurried to the theater—storekeepers and their wives, and many boys who worked as shop helpers. Rich lords came on horseback. Other people crossed the river on small ferryboats.

Some people paid a penny to enter the theater. They were called groundlings. For this penny they could stand on the ground floor in an open space around three sides of the stage. Those who paid two pennies could buy seats in one of the three rows of galleries that lined the walls of the theater. For rich noblemen who paid 12 pennies, there were more comfortable seats in the gentlemen's boxes. At other theaters of that day, like the Rose and the Fortune, people also sat on the stage during the play.

There was no artificial lighting in these semi-outdoor theaters, and the daylight streaming in through the open roof provided the only light to see by. Also, there were no printed programs and no scenery, so the actors had to set the scene with their words and with movable props. The audience understood that the scene was taking place at night when a man carrying a torch appeared on the stage. Lines like " 'Tis now struck twelve" and " 'Tis bitter cold" set the scene.

There was no curtain at the front of the stage. Actors walked off at the side exit when the scene ended. More actors entered immediately to start the next scene. If someone died as part of the plot, devices were written into the play to get the body off the stage. Otherwise, the actor would have had to lie there for the whole performance.

At the back of the stage there was an alcove that was curtained off. This inner stage was used when characters needed to hide, or to appear suddenly. Also scenes requiring a large prop, such as a throne, were played in the alcove. Another alcove above the lower one, was called the chamber, and was used for scenes when the play called for one character to be above the others, as if on the walls of a city or on a balcony. Juliet played the balcony scenes from *Romeo and Juliet* from the chamber. This upper stage was also curtained.

Since women did not act on the stage in

The Globe Theater in London was an eight-sided building, three stories high, and lighted only by daylight coming through the open center.

Some earlier theaters were made by blocking off a street and building a platform for a stage.

Shakespeare's time, their parts were played by young boys. These boys were expertly made up and acted so well that they seemed feminine.

The theater was so popular in Shakespeare's England that it became a big business. Shakespeare was a member of the company that presented the plays at the Globe—many of which he had written—and he shared in the profits and became rich. Other playwrights who were not members of a company were not so lucky. They sold their works to the companies outright, and they received only about 30 dollars for a full-length play.

Sometimes a company sold a popular play to a printer who published it as a small book. Some of Shakespeare's plays, such as *Richard III*, were published often. Others, such as *Macbeth*, were not published during his lifetime.

Although theaters like the Globe were the biggest and best attended, smaller indoor theaters grew up early in the 17th century. Here the companies played during the winter when they could not play at the larger, open-roofed theaters. Blackfriars was the name of the indoor theater where Shakespeare's company performed. There were fewer seats and artificial lighting was required. The tickets were therefore more expensive, and only wealthy people could afford to attend.

Sometimes the players performed at court for Queen Elizabeth and her successor, King James I. Shakespeare's *The Merry Wives of Windsor* was probably performed at Windsor Castle before Queen Elizabeth as part of a wedding celebration. Almost all of the plays were written in a particular unrhymed, rhythmic poetry called blank verse. The acting companies that performed the plays did not put on the same show every night. They were called repertory companies, and they would perform a whole group of plays in one season, playing different plays on different days.

The audiences liked their plays to seem realistic. If there was a shipwreck in the play, the survivors had to enter the stage wet. In many of the historical plays real guns and cannons were fired backstage. When Shakespeare's *Henry VIII* was playing at the Globe in 1613, a gun was fired as King Henry made an important entrance. A spark from the gun went into the thatched roof. The fire spread quickly and the Globe burned to the ground.

According to Sir Henry Wotton, who was there, only one person was hurt in the fire. "Only one man had his breeches set on fire, that would perhaps have broiled him, if he had not by the benefit of a provident wit put it out with bottle ale."

In battle scenes, such as this one from Macbeth, an effect of clashing swords and shouts of fighting men came from behind the scenes.

Scenes *like the balcony scene in* Romeo and Juliet (*above*) *were played on the balconies that were built into the sides and back of the stage.*

The women in The Merry Wives of Windsor (*below*) *were played by young men who moved so gracefully that they actually seemed to be women.*

Belgium was under Austrian rule for most of the 18th century. A Belgian revolt in 1790 was severely crushed, and the Austrians themselves were soon afterwards defeated by the French.

were discontented under Spanish rule, and they began a struggle for liberty and religious freedom. The struggle came to the boiling point when Charles V passed the rule of the combined countries to his son, Philip II of Spain. The war against the tyranny of Spain by the people of Holland lasted nearly 100 years. During the fighting, the Dutch even flooded their own country to drive the Spanish out. The struggle at first was inspired and organized by a prince of the House of Orange known as William the Silent. Even his murder by the Spanish in 1584 did not discourage the Netherlanders.

Holland and Belgium separated in 1585, Catholic Belgium remaining with Spain. The Dutch won their independence in the Treaty of Westphalia in 1648. During the years of oppression and desperate fighting, they also managed to become masters of the seas and the greatest trading nation in the world.

THE NETHERLANDS
AREA: *12,850 square miles*
POP: *11,173,000*
CAPITAL: *Amsterdam*
RELIGIONS: *Netherlands Reformed Church, Roman Catholic*
LANGUAGE: *Dutch*
MONETARY UNIT: *Guilder (26.32¢)*
BELGIUM
AREA: *11,775 square miles*
POP: *9,104,000*
CAPITAL: *Brussels*
RELIGIONS: *Roman Catholic, Jewish, Church of England, Protestant Evangelical*
LANGUAGES: *French, Flemish*
MONETARY UNIT: *Franc (2¢)*

The Dutch East India Company was formed at the beginning of the 17th century and became fabulously rich. Its trading activities led to the founding of the Dutch East Indian empire and to two naval wars with England. Later, Holland joined with England to fight France in a war that ended in 1713. But as other

The Low Countries in the second half of the 16th century

Legend:
- The Netherlands
- Belgium and Luxemburg
- Neighboring countries

FRIESLAND

DRENTHE

Zuider Zee

Zwolle

OVERYSSEL

Haarlem

Amsterdam

Utrecht

GELDERLAND

The Hague

HOLLAND

Arnheim

Rotterdam

North Sea

Breda

Antwerp

BRABANTE

Bruges

Ghent

FLANDERS

LIEGE

LIMBURG

Ypres

Lille

Brussels

Tournai

Liege

ARTOIS

HAINAUT

Namur

Arras

NAMUR

LUXEMBURG

Luxemburg

William of Orange inspired and organized the Low Countries' rebellion against Spanish rule.

countries became more powerful. Dutch power dwindled.

By treaties in 1713 and 1715 Belgium came under Austrian rule. A Belgian revolt in 1790 was crushed, and two years later the Austrians repelled a French invasion.

However, in 1794 the Low Countries were overrun by the French army. The ruling Orange family escaped, and the two provinces were made part of the French Empire. When Napoleon was defeated in 1814, the House of Orange returned to power. The northern and southern provinces were made the Kingdom of the Netherlands. However, the union of the northern Protestant Dutch and the southern Catholic Belgians was not satisfactory. In 1830 Belgium withdrew and formed its own kingdom.

Holland kept her many colonies until recently. In 1949 Indonesia became independent, and in 1954 the South American and West Indian colonies of Surinam, the Antilles, and Dutch New Guinea were given equal status to the Netherlands homeland within the Kingdom of the Netherlands.

At the end of the 19th century, Belgium set out to explore parts of Africa. The king, Leopold II, became sovereign of the new territory, called the Congo Free State, which he bequeathed to Belgium. The Belgian Congo colonies were officially ceded to Belgium in 1908. These colonies remained under the con-

Belgian kings

Albert I, 1909 to 1934   *Leopold III, 1934 to 1951*   *Baudouin I, since 1951*

The Belgian Congo was a colony from 1908 until 1960, when it became independent.

Dikes are built along the seacoast and riverbanks to keep the land from being flooded. Almost 40 percent of the Netherlands and the west coast of the Netherlands and Belgium are below sea level.

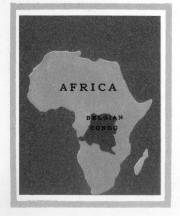

trol of Belgium until 1960, when they gained their independence.

In World War I, the Netherlands and Belgium remained neutral, but Belgium was invaded by Germany. Both countries were occupied by the Germans in World War II, in spite of their desire to be neutral.

Today both the Netherlands and Belgium, because their drainage canal system can also be used for irrigation, are rich agricultural countries. But, though they are tied together geographically and historically, each kingdom has its individual character.

The Netherlands is not as big as Massachusetts and Connecticut combined. Its capital is Amsterdam, but its government is in The Hague. Its population is predominantly Protestant. The country is flat and veined by canals. The farmers raise cattle and sell dairy products and tulip bulbs, which were originally imported from Persia. The Dutch fields are marvelously colorful in the spring when the tulips are in bloom. Not many of the flowers are sold, but the bulbs are dug up and shipped all over the world. The Netherlands is also a country of craftsmen who specialize in shipbuilding, diamond cutting, machine manufacturing, pottery, and electrical and radio equipment.

Belgium, which is smaller than the Netherlands, is the second most densely populated country in Europe. Its people are divided into two groups, the Walloons, who speak French, and the Flemish, whose language has developed from the Dutch. Both languages are spoken officially. Most Belgians are Roman Catholics. Belgium's great cities, such as Bruges, Ghent, Brussels, and Antwerp, grew up and thrived in the Middle Ages. They are famous for their art works and architecture. Although part of the country is agricultural, the central section of Belgium, where there are iron, zinc, lead, copper, and coal mines, is industrial. Even the sand from Belgium's dunes is used—in making glass. For centuries Belgian women have been famous for their lace making. And carpets which are known as Brussels carpets, although they are made at Tournai, are exported all over the world.

Crabs

The common crab, shown in the illustration, has a shell, called a carapace, which is formed by a secretion from the skin of the animal (1). This crab has two pairs of sensitive antennae, which are its organs for feeling and smelling (2). The common crab has a single jaw (3) and two pairs of additional jaws (4). There are also three pairs of foot jaws, called maxillipedes, which the crab uses to put food into its mouth (5). Its eyes are set on the top of two movable stalks. If the stalks are removed from the crab, the animal can grow new ones (6). The crab uses its five pairs of legs for walking. The first pair of feet has the shape of claws and is used by the crab as hands and as weapons. The crab uses the claws to catch its prey or to grab hold of the marine plants which it puts on top of its shell to camouflage itself (7). The crab's gills, the organs it uses for breathing under water, are in a hollow at the base of the thorax and are covered by the shell (8). The gills are shaped like small feathers arranged in many rows.

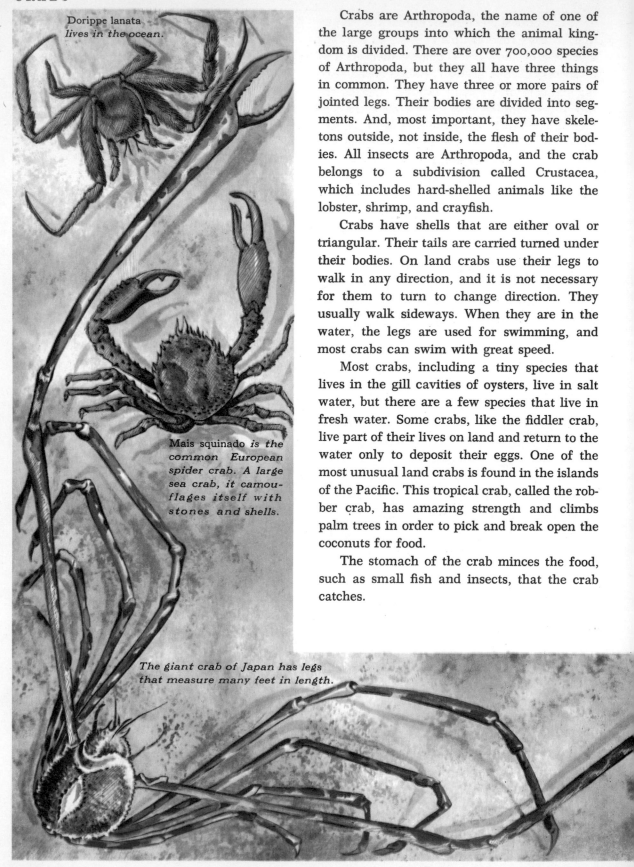

Dorippe lanata *lives in the ocean.*

Mais squinado *is the common European spider crab. A large sea crab, it camouflages itself with stones and shells.*

The giant crab of Japan has legs that measure many feet in length.

Crabs are Arthropoda, the name of one of the large groups into which the animal kingdom is divided. There are over 700,000 species of Arthropoda, but they all have three things in common. They have three or more pairs of jointed legs. Their bodies are divided into segments. And, most important, they have skeletons outside, not inside, the flesh of their bodies. All insects are Arthropoda, and the crab belongs to a subdivision called Crustacea, which includes hard-shelled animals like the lobster, shrimp, and crayfish.

Crabs have shells that are either oval or triangular. Their tails are carried turned under their bodies. On land crabs use their legs to walk in any direction, and it is not necessary for them to turn to change direction. They usually walk sideways. When they are in the water, the legs are used for swimming, and most crabs can swim with great speed.

Most crabs, including a tiny species that lives in the gill cavities of oysters, live in salt water, but there are a few species that live in fresh water. Some crabs, like the fiddler crab, live part of their lives on land and return to the water only to deposit their eggs. One of the most unusual land crabs is found in the islands of the Pacific. This tropical crab, called the robber crab, has amazing strength and climbs palm trees in order to pick and break open the coconuts for food.

The stomach of the crab minces the food, such as small fish and insects, that the crab catches.

The crab's shell does not grow with the animal, so from time to time it becomes too tight and must be shed. Crabs change their shell by a process called molting. The shell opens, leaving the skin of the crab exposed. During the time it takes for the shell to grow back, the crab hides among rocks or at the bottom of the sea. After a few days the new shell is formed and the crab comes out of hiding.

In the United States soft-shell crabs, found all along the Atlantic coast, are considered a delicacy. They are blue crabs caught just before they molt and kept in floats until the old shell is shed.

A few years ago a scientist performed a cruel but interesting experiment. He placed a living crab on a fire. The animal jumped away, leaving his 10 feet in the fire. All crabs can lose their feet, claws, and eye stalks and grow them back again. When two crabs fight, the loser may leave its feet in the pincers of its enemy. After the next molting period the loser will have regrown all its feet.

Crabs are found in sizes ranging from three quarters of an inch to almost 14 feet between outstretched feet. The giant crab of Japan is said to measure nearly 13½ feet between its extended claws, and the morro crab of Cuba weighs up to 12 pounds and has very powerful claws.

It is difficult to measure how intelligent an animal is, but crabs seem to act with intelli-

Some crabs use sea anemones, which have stinging tentacles, as weapons.

gence. Some of them, for example, place a sea anemone, armed with stinging tentacles, on their shells as a guard. When these crabs fight they hold the sea anemone in their pincers and wave it about as a weapon.

Crabs reproduce by laying eggs. The female crab lays thousands of tiny eggs, usually in winter. The eggs hatch into larvae which grow and change their shape while floating in the water. Several times before they become adult they molt. With each molt, the crab rises to the surface and floats until the new shell is formed. Then it sinks again to the bottom. This process continues until at adulthood the crab remains at the bottom.

Dromia vulgaris, which is often called the porter crab, carries a sponge on its back.

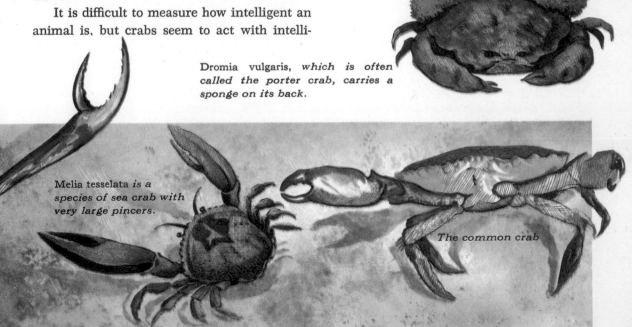

Melia tesselata is a species of sea crab with very large pincers.

The common crab

CRABS

Crabs, like many other shellfish, are eaten in large quantities by people all over the world, so catching shellfish is a big business which earns money for shellfishermen the world over. In one year commercial fishermen in the United States caught over 100,000,000 pounds of crab. Crabs, like lobster and crayfish, are caught in baited traps and are sold either fresh, boiled, canned, or frozen.

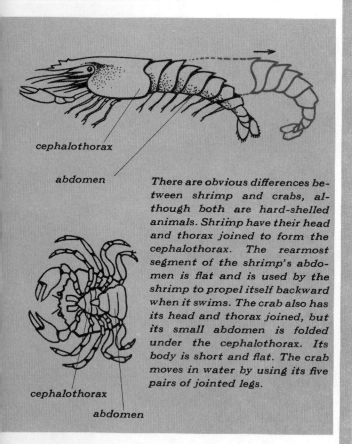

cephalothorax

abdomen

There are obvious differences between shrimp and crabs, although both are hard-shelled animals. Shrimp have their head and thorax joined to form the cephalothorax. The rearmost segment of the shrimp's abdomen is flat and is used by the shrimp to propel itself backward when it swims. The crab also has its head and thorax joined, but its small abdomen is folded under the cephalothorax. Its body is short and flat. The crab moves in water by using its five pairs of jointed legs.

cephalothorax

abdomen

The larvae of the crab develop and change their shape while floating in the water.

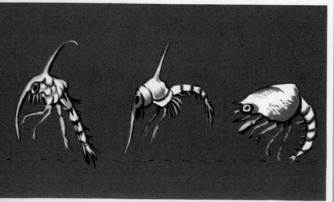

Tools of Stone Age Man

Primitive man was different from his apelike ancestors in two important ways—his ability to make tools, and his ability to walk upright on two feet. Scientists are not sure whether he learned to walk upright first and then made tools for himself, or whether it was the other way around. But once early man learned to stand upright, his hands were free to use the tools he made. Probably as long as 1,000,000 years ago man used stones as tools to pound, dig, and scrape with.

In general, Stone Age tools are divided into two periods—the Old Stone Age, or Paleolithic period of unpolished flints, and the New Stone Age, or Neolithic period of finished and polished stone tools. Within these two periods there were many different types of tools.

The earliest implements were simply stones that happened to be suitably shaped for use as tools. Sometimes they were crudely chipped to improve their shape, but usually they were used just as they were found. These ancient tools are called eoliths, or dawn tools.

As man progressed through successive stages, he modified the natural shape of the stones to make his implements more useful.

There were many different ways of making tools from stone. Plain stone, which archeologists call the nodule, was used in the dawn tools. Then gradually man learned the skill of hammering the stone in such a way as to break off a splinter from it. This small piece is called a flake, and the tools and weapons made from it are called flake tools. The remainder of the stone is known as the core. Tools made from it are called core tools. As man developed, he learned to chip the edges of the flake or core tool to sharpen them. Still later he learned to place a sharp tool against the stone he was shaping and to flake chips off it by pressure. This is called pressure flaking.

One of the oldest known groups of man—Peking man—may have been able to slightly modify the shape of the rocks he wanted to use as tools. A partly burned deer's antler found with some of his tools make scientists believe that even Peking man may have used the bone to chip flakes off the nodule stones.

Pre-Chellean, or Early Chellean tools, named for the town of Chelles, France, where a variety of them were found, were core tools, selected for their natural shape. One end was used as the handle, and flakes were struck off the other end to give it a rough edge. The Chelleans also made a few crude flake tools.

Nodule stones of the Peking man

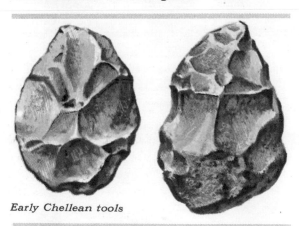

Early Chellean tools

Later Chellean tools   *Hand scraper*

The later Chelleans struck flakes off both ends of the nodules to make an almond shaped tool. These tools were probably used as knives,

scrapers, and borers. The Chelleans also made other tools, such as hand scrapers, which were probably used to cure animal skins, and they made tools for punching holes.

A Chellean punch tool

The next major stage of tool development is known as the Acheulian Age. This age is named for St. Acheul, France, where tools that were used by the earlier Neanderthal men were first discovered. Like the Chellean, the Acheulian tools were chipped on both sides, and wooden handles were often tied to them with cord made of animal intestines.

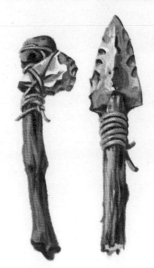

Acheulian tools

Mousterian tool of Neanderthal man

Later on, Neanderthal man used Mousterian tools, first found in the French cave Le Moustier. The Mousterian Neanderthals were able to chip their tools more precisely and to get a sharper edge on them. They used bone handles on some tools. Bones were also used as scrapers.

TOOLS OF STONE AGE MAN

During the time of Cro-Magnon man, many new skills in the making of weapons and tools were developed. Cro-Magnon implements are divided into three eras. Each era takes its name from the place where the tools in it were found. The first was the Aurignacian. The Aurignacians knew how to make notched tools. They gradually learned to tie a saw-edged stone to a bone handle and, eventually, to insert stone teeth into the handle itself, fastening them to it with resin.

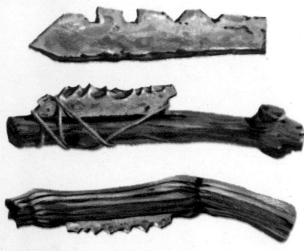

Aurignacian notched tools

During the second Cro-Magnon stage—the Solutrean—man learned to make what is called the laurel leaf weapon. It is made with the use of a burin—a long sharp pointed tool that could also be used for engraving. With the burin, flakes were chipped off by pressure, leaving a leaf-shaped stone with a thin, sharp edge.

Solutrean tool   *A Solutrean spear tip*

The third Cro-Magnon period is called the Magdalenian Age. During this time stone was used less and less. Stones were still used as hammers and anvils, but most tools and weapons were made of bone. Among the implements Cro-Magnon man made were bone needles with eyes in them for the thongs that were used as

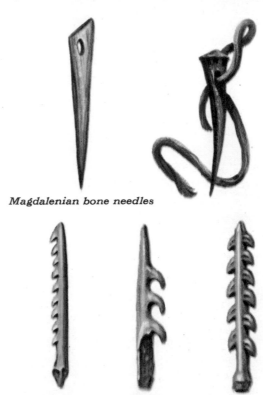

Magdalenian bone needles

Magdalenian bone harpoon and spear points

Cro-Magnon arrowheads

Azilian bone fishhooks   *Net-making tool*

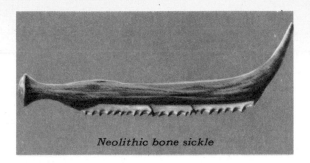

Neolithic bone sickle

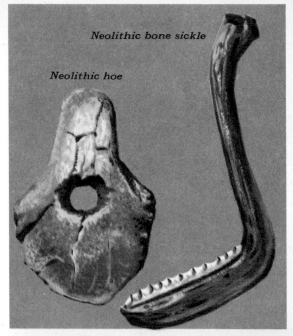

Neolithic bone sickle

Neolithic hoe

thread. In the Magdalenian period men also made notched harpoons and ornamented their spear points with engravings.

During the three stages of Cro-Magnon workmanship, the arrowhead progressed from a crude flake object to a well designed piece that could be easily bound to a wooden shaft.

During the transition period from the early to the late Stone Age, man learned to make nets and to fish for his food. Fishhooks of bone have been found dating from the period of the Azilians, one of the cultural groups that existed during this period.

In the New Stone Age, or Neolithic Age, man learned to polish his stone weapons by grinding or by very fine chipping. He also developed a drill for boring holes. Then Neolithic man began to settle in one place, and this period saw the beginning of farming. A stone hoe had a hole into which a wooden handle could be inserted. A straight sickle was made of bone with flint teeth fastened along its edge with resin. A more elaborate, practical sickle had a curved wooden handle, much the same shape as our modern tool.

During the Cro-Magnon era, man shaped his flint tools by a process called pressure flaking.

A cave painting of the Cro-Magnon period shows that these early men used bows and arrows.

with other forms of dress, reached their extreme in ornamental and fanciful styling.

In America, there were shoemakers from the earliest times. Shoemaker Thomas Beard came here on the *Mayflower*. Eventually, all the colonies had shoemakers, but New England remained a leader in shoe manufacturing.

Gradually, during the 19th century, machine manufacture of shoes came to replace the individual shoemaker. Early in the century various machine methods were developed for attaching the sole to the upper. In the 1850's the McKay stitching machine was invented. This mechanized the laborious process of stitching together the inner and outer soles, and was an extremely important development in the shoe industry. Throughout the century many new important devices and methods were developed for simplifying, improving, and standardizing shoe manufacture.

There are a number of machine methods used in making various types of shoes. One that has been in use a long time is still the most popular. It is the Goodyear welt process. This process consists of three basic operations: the cutting of the uppers, the cutting of the soles, and the assembling, or putting together, of the two parts. Each of these operations has been broken down into each of its many steps to take full advantage of assembly line methods. The cutting is done by great machines which have cut surfaces shaped in the pattern desired to be cut. Assembling the uppers, soles, and heels involves stitching, tacking, nailing, and cementing. The assembling is done on a last, a block made in the shape of a foot.

The leather to be used in making shoes must be chosen with care. The method of tanning and finishing that is used will influence the comfort and wearability of the shoes to be

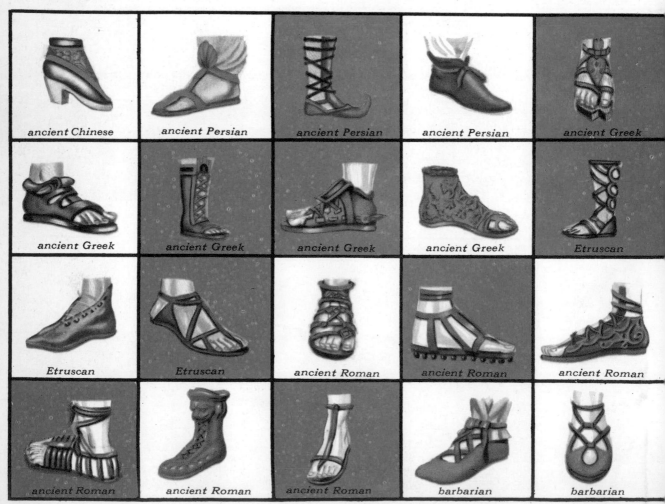

ancient Chinese | ancient Persian | ancient Persian | ancient Persian | ancient Greek

ancient Greek | ancient Greek | ancient Greek | ancient Greek | Etruscan

Etruscan | Etruscan | ancient Roman | ancient Roman | ancient Roman

ancient Roman | ancient Roman | ancient Roman | barbarian | barbarian

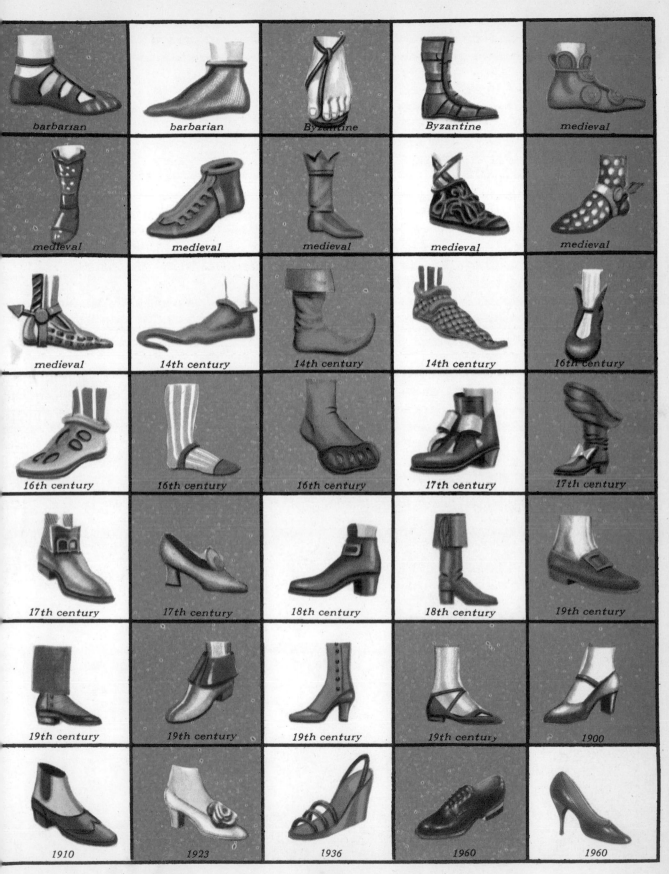

barbarian | barbarian | Byzantine | Byzantine | medieval

medieval | medieval | medieval | medieval | medieval

medieval | 14th century | 14th century | 14th century | 16th century

16th century | 16th century | 16th century | 17th century | 17th century

17th century | 17th century | 18th century | 18th century | 19th century

19th century | 19th century | 19th century | 19th century | 1900

1910 | 1923 | 1936 | 1960 | 1960

made from it. Shoe soles are generally made of cattle hide, although many of them are also made of compositions of rubber and synthetics. For the upper part of heavy shoes, cattle hide is used. The upper part of lighter shoes is made from calfskin, pigskin, goatskin, or lighter cattle hides.

It is only since the first World War, 1914-1918, that shoe manufacturers have been concerned with style and variety in shoes. Before that time, both men's and women's shoes had been designed primarily to be useful.

The major centers of shoe manufacture in the United States include New England, New York State, and St. Louis, Missouri.

The United States is the major manufacturer of the machinery used in making shoes throughout the world. Today, handiwork is done only in the repairing of shoes and in making shoes to order.

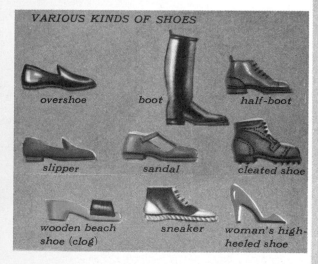

VARIOUS KINDS OF SHOES

overshoe   boot   half-boot

slipper   sandal   cleated shoe

wooden beach shoe (clog)   sneaker   woman's high-heeled shoe

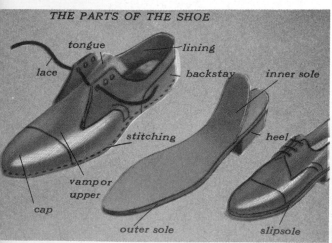

THE PARTS OF THE SHOE

tongue   lining

lace   backstay   inner sole

stitching   heel

vamp or upper

cap

outer sole   slipsole

Types of Roots

The roots of plants usually grow downward in the ground. But some plants have their roots in water or in the air. Orchids, for example, have only aerial roots. They cling to the stems of other plants or to the branches of trees.

Roots have several functions. They anchor or hold the plant in place, and they help to keep it upright. Through tiny projections called root hairs, roots absorb water and minerals from the soil. These pass into the main part of the root and are conducted up the stem. Some roots also store a reserve supply of food.

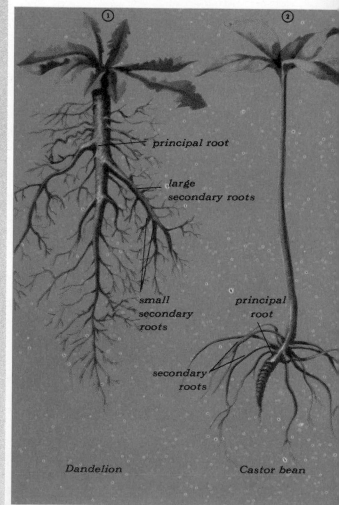

principal root

large secondary roots

small secondary roots

secondary roots

principal root

Dandelion   Castor bean

UNDERGROUND ROOTS

The two main kinds of underground roots are taproots and branching or fibrous roots. A taproot grows down directly from the stem. It is larger than any of the secondary roots that grow from it. It goes deep into the ground without dividing. Dandelion taproots often grow to be more than three feet long (1).

A branching root is a tuft of thick primary roots which does not extend deep into the ground. The root of the castor bean is an example of this kind of shallow, thick root (2).

Some taproots are thick and fleshy and can be eaten. Carrots (3), radishes, beets, and turnips are edible taproots. Such taproots hold the plant in place, store a reserve of food substances for the plant, and supply water, which is absorbed through the root hairs and then into the plant.

ADVENTITIOUS ROOTS

Adventitious roots grow out of the stem or leaves or branches of the plant. Plants with adventitious roots usually need more support for their stems. In cereal plants, such as corn (4), the principal root is almost dead and the vital roots have grown out of the stem of the plant.

The mangrove tree (5), which grows in warm, marshy areas, has a main root that decays in muddy soil. After this occurs, roots grow into the sand from the branches above.

The banyan tree (6) has long, heavy branches which send out aerial roots that first hang free and eventually root in the ground. These roots become large and strong in order to support the branches and eventually these branches become trunk-like. A single banyan tree may develop quickly into a grove of trees because of the way its aerial roots spread.

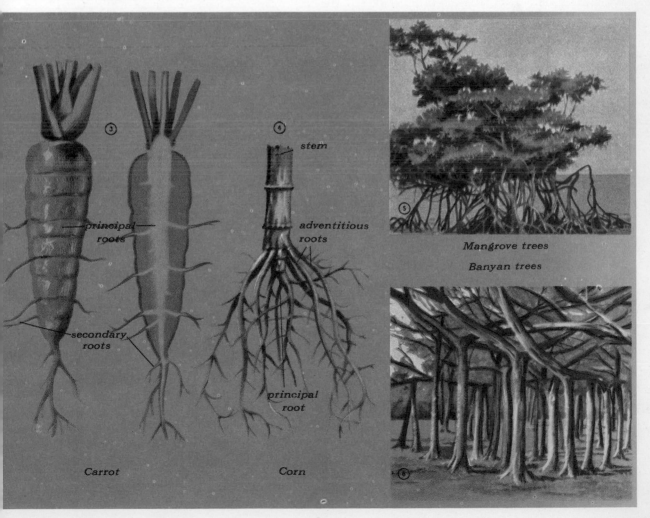

principal roots

secondary roots

stem

adventitious roots

principal root

Carrot

Corn

Mangrove trees

Banyan trees

The Mighty Atom—Its Power

The idea of atomic energy usually calls to mind radioactivity, the atomic bomb, or the atomic reactor. These three aspects of atomic science are all related.

In 1896, the French physicist Henri Becquerel discovered that certain uranium compounds would fog or expose a photographic film, even though the film was carefully kept away from light. He found that these compounds also glowed in the dark. Intrigued by Becquerel's discoveries, Pierre and Marie Curie did more research in this area and obtained similar results with thorium and radium. What these scientists had discovered is now known as radioactivity.

There are three types of radioactive radiation—alpha and beta particles and gamma rays. Alpha particles are simply the free nuclei of helium atoms. Like all atomic nuclei, they are positively charged. Beta particles are negatively charged since they are single, free electrons. Gamma rays are electromagnetic radiations similar in nature to light, x-rays, or radio waves (1).

When an atom gives up or radiates a part of itself, its character changes. Radium has an atomic weight of 226. An alpha particle, the helium nucleus, has an atomic weight of 4. Thus the radium atom loses four units of atomic weight when it emits an alpha particle. Its new atomic weight is only 222, and the new substance with this weight is no longer radium, but a rare gas called radon (2). Radon itself will emit more particles. This process of radioactive decay will continue until the non-radioactive element lead is reached. This lead has an atomic weight of 206. It is an isotope of ordinary lead of atomic weight 207. Isotopes have the same chemical properties as ordinary atoms but different atomic weights and physical properties.

The alpha particles are thrown out of atoms at tremendous speeds. In 1919, the English physicist Lord Rutherford used alpha particles much as bullets shot out of a gun. His gun consisted of a piece of radium that was enclosed

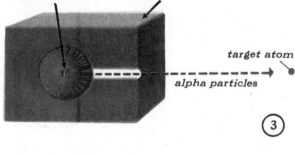

RADIUM

RADIUM
alpha particles
beta particles
gamma rays
(1)

atom of radium — 226
alpha particle — 4
atom of radon — 222
(2)

fragment of radium   block of lead
target atom
alpha particles
(3)

in a block of lead which had a small hole in it through which the alpha particles passed (3). Later devices, such as the betatron or synchrotron, have improved upon Rutherford's process. Such huge machines focus and speed up the atomic particles. They shoot the particles into the center of a target atom to help scientists learn more about its structure.

In 1932, another English scientist, James Chadwick, discovered a new particle inside the atom called the neutron. The neutron has about the same mass as the proton and, like the proton, is found in the nucleus of the atom. Unlike the proton, however, the neutron is electrically neutral and has neither a positive nor a

The nucleus of the helium atom contains two protons and two neutrons.

negative charge. As a result, the number of neutrons does not depend upon the number of electrons or protons. The radium atom, for example, has 88 electrons, 88 protons, and 138 neutrons.

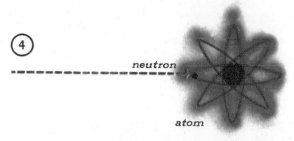

④ neutron

atom

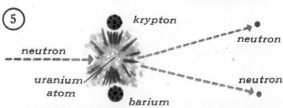

⑤ krypton

neutron

neutron

uranium atom

neutron

barium

The discovery of the neutron was very important because it gave scientists another tool for investigating the atom. When used as a bullet, the alpha particle, being electrically charged, can be bent in its path. But the neutron is more like an armor-piercing shell. Because it is electrically neutral, the neutron can penetrate to the heart of an atomic nucleus (4). Neutron bombardment can create new elements when neutrons are captured by a nucleus.

THE ATOM BOMB

In 1938, an atom of uranium was split in two by two German scientists, Otto Hahn and Fritz Strassman. In 1940, the United States started its research to produce an atomic bomb.

The splitting of uranium was a major step forward because the uranium atom splits into two almost equal parts—such as barium and krypton—when struck by a neutron (5). Alpha particles had only been able to chip small pieces off the atom. Now the atom was split into two large pieces by a process known as nuclear fission.

In breaking up, the uranium nucleus emits two or more additional neutrons. These in turn may hit other uranium nuclei, which can split and release yet more neutrons. When this splitting process continues, it results in what is known as a chain reaction (6).

Tremendous forces hold an atom of uranium together. When it is split, these forces are released. The fission of one pound of uranium would give as much energy as 20,000,000 pounds of coal. If a large amount of uranium undergoes nuclear fission at the same time, a vast amount of energy is released in a fraction of a second. In an atomic bomb, billions of nuclei are split in an instantaneous chain reaction, releasing more billions of neutrons, and producing a temperature of millions of degrees. It is one of the most destructive forces known to man.

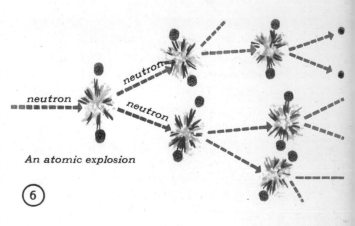

neutron

neutron

neutron

An atomic explosion

⑥

THE ATOMIC REACTOR

An atomic explosion is a tremendous source of power, but it need not always be destructive. Man has been able to slow down the splitting of the atom to produce what is known as controlled fission. Controlled fission describes the kind of atom splitting that takes place in an atomic reactor or atomic pile. The first atomic pile went into operation on December 2, 1942. On this date Enrico Fermi, an Italian physicist, working with a group of American scientists at the University of Chicago, achieved the first controlled nuclear chain reaction.

An atomic pile has three principal parts. A shield protects observers from the radioactivity inside the pile and is usually made of concrete or lead. Radioactive fuel is often in the form of rods of uranium. Control rods are usually made of boron or cadmium, which are not radioactive and can absorb free neutrons, much as a sponge absorbs drops of water.

It is the free neutrons that cause an atomic chain reaction, and it is the job of the control rods to regulate the number of free neutrons. When the rods are pushed all the way into the atomic pile, most of the neutrons are absorbed in the boron and cadmium, and little splitting of uranium atoms takes place. As the rods are pulled out of the pile, however, more and more neutrons can reach the uranium nuclei. The nuclei in turn release still more neutrons, and a chain reaction results. If the chain reaction goes too quickly, the rods can be pushed back into the pile, so that there is no danger of an atomic explosion.

The atomic reactor produces great amounts of heat as the uranium atoms are split. The pieces of atoms travel at great speed until they are stopped by other atoms in the pile. It is the stopping which creates heat, just as metal will become hot when it is beaten with a hammer.

This heat energy must be taken out of the reactor for man to be able to use it. Usually a liquid—either water under pressure or a liquid metal, such as an alloy of sodium and potassium—is circulated in tubes inside the reactor. This liquid is greatly heated by the reaction. It then passes into a boiler where it heats water

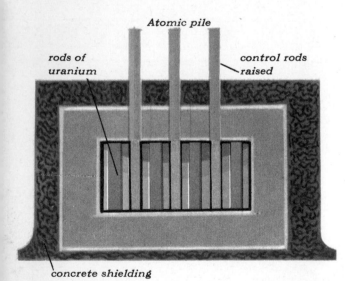

rods of uranium   Atomic pile   control rods lowered

concrete shielding

Atomic pile

rods of uranium   control rods raised

concrete shielding

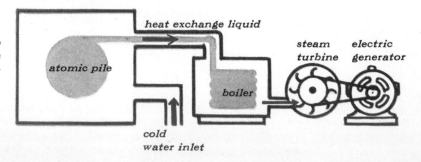

An atomic engine works like other engines, except that its source of energy is atomic fission instead of coal or oil.

heat exchange liquid

atomic pile

steam turbine   electric generator

boiler

cold water inlet

This cross-section shows the inside of an atomic bomb. A mush-room-shaped cloud of deadly gases follows the bomb's explosion.

to steam. The steam can then be used to drive a turbine which can drive an electrical generator.

All atomic engines operate on this same principle. A liquid heated inside the reactor is used to heat water to steam. The engine of the atomic submarine *Nautilus* works in the same way. The heat exchange liquid used in this submarine is water under pressure. The control rods are made of hafnium, a metal discovered in 1932. The water has to be kept under pres-

sure or it will flash into steam inside the reactor itself and the usable heat will be lost. With a few pounds of uranium, the submarine can travel for months without being refueled.

Atomic reactors can also be used on land to produce electrical power for industry and homes. Twenty pounds of uranium could light 25,000 homes for one year. At present, the electricity produced by atomic power plants is not cheap, but as the cost becomes lower and as

Atomic powered submarine

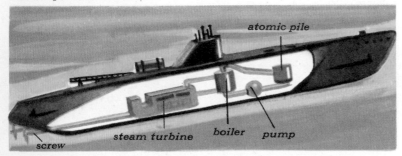

atomic pile

steam turbine *boiler* *pump*

screw

 H

 H

Atomic fusion occurs when two atoms of hydrogen (H) combine to form an atom of helium (He), releasing tremendous energy.

The U. S. Navy submarine Nautilus *is powered by an atomic engine.*

coal and oil become harder to obtain, atomic energy will become one of man's greatest power sources. Even more exciting is the possibility that in the near future man will learn how to control thermonuclear reactions in which atoms of hydrogen join together to form an atom of helium, with the release of tremendous energy. This is not atomic fission, but atomic fusion, and it is the source of the heat of the sun itself.

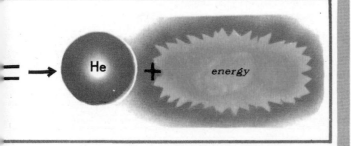

The first full-scale atomic power plant in the world was established in England in 1956.

Desert Animals

Only a small number of animals are capable of living under the extreme conditions found in deserts, where there is little or no rainfall and the temperatures vary greatly from day to night.

Some desert animals get liquid from the blood of other animals or from the plants they eat. Some are able to survive without water for long periods of time. Many live near oases, water holes where vegetation grows. The water may come up from a spring or, if the area is high enough, it may receive a small amount of rainfall.

Desert animals are usually sand-colored or gray-green, and blend in with their background. This protective coloring, a natural camouflage, hides them from their enemies and is one way they are able to protect themselves in places where there is little shelter.

There are many kinds of birds in the desert. They feed on insects and small rodents. Large birds, such as the ostrich, emu, and vulture, live in the African deserts. In the American deserts there are eagles, owls, roadrunners, woodpeckers, mocking birds, doves, sparrows, and many other birds.

The heat of the desert and the abundance of insects make it an ideal place for reptiles to live. Desert insects are numerous. Birds, snakes, and lizards eat them. Most of them are wingless ones, such as ants and crickets.

Other desert animals include the jack rabbit, cottontail, mountain lion, gopher, and Gila monster. (See pages 1180 and 1181.)

(1) The pack rat is a small bushy-tailed rodent. It is named for its habit of collecting little things that suit its fancy and taking them home to its nest. The pack rat sleeps in the daytime and goes out at night to hunt for seeds and mesquite beans.

(2) The kangaroo rat hops like a kangaroo on long hind legs and short front ones. It lives on seeds that it carries in the fur-lined pouch

(9) The horned toad is really a lizard. It has a flattened body with spines on it. It catches insects on the glue-covered tip of its tongue. The horned toad is sluggish and harmless and protects itself by hiding under prickly vegetation. Its eggs hatch an hour after being laid. Baby horned toads are able to take care of themselves as soon as they are born.

(10) The desert snail is found in the African deserts. It comes out of its shell only during a rainstorm.

(11) The agama is a lizard which changes color with the seasons. In the summer it is a greenish orange and in the winter it is brown. It lives almost entirely on the fruit of date palms found in the oases. Agamas are eaten by some Africans.

(12) The owl sleeps in the daytime and hunts at night. It lives on small rodents, lizards, and insects.

(1) *The cricket lives in the Sahara. It digs branching burrows deep underground.*

(2) *The dung beetle lays its eggs in the dung of other animals.*

(3) *The sand termite lives on the cellulose of treewood, leaves, roots, and twigs*

The Suez Canal

The Suez Canal is a waterway 107 miles long including the approaches. It crosses Egypt from the Mediterranean to the Red Sea, cutting through the isthmus that joins Asia and Africa. The canal is 42.5 feet deep. Its width at the bottom is 197 feet. Since the surfaces of the Mediterranean and the Red seas are at about the same level, the Suez Canal needs no locks to raise or lower ships from one water level to another.

A pilot boards all ships to guide them on the 12 to 15 hour trip through the canal. Some parts of the canal can only handle one-way traffic. On the Mediterranean end of the canal is the city of Port Said. The canal enters the Red Sea at the city of Suez. Desert sands that are constantly blown into the canal fill it up, so there are always dredges working to clear the bottom.

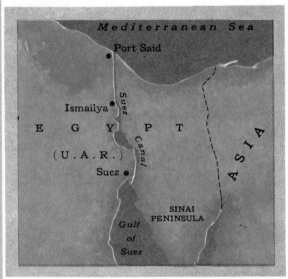

The Suez Canal connects the Mediterranean with the Red Sea.

The idea of a canal joining the Mediterranean with the Red Sea is an old one, and nobody knows when the first canal was built in this area. However, the need was recognized as early as the 20th century B.C., and there is an Egyptian inscription that indicates that a canal existed as long ago as 1380 B.C., and probably before that.

Various Egyptian pharaohs had the canal re-dug from time to time, but it was constantly filling up again. In 520 B.C. the Persian King Darius improved the Egyptian canal, which at this time reached only from the Mediterranean to the Bitter Lakes. For some time goods were carried this far by boat, and then carried by land the remaining distance to the Red Sea.

Darius built his canal on a waterway that later dried up. Later, the Roman Emperor Trajan started a new canal that in many parts followed the course of the present-day waterway. When Egypt became part of the Arab Empire, the canal was improved and extended by the Arabs.

In A.D. 770, a Mohammedan caliph closed the canal to prevent his enemies from getting supplies by this route. It was reopened later, but in 1811 Mohammed Ali, another Arab ruler, ordered it closed again. By this time, the Nile River floods and the constantly blowing sand had already blocked up many parts of it.

When Europeans began to trade with the Far East, they became interested in building a canal across Egypt. By using a Suez waterway, a ship could save over 5,000 miles on the trip from London to Bombay, India. Obviously such a short cut was vitally important to the people of Europe. Many people considered building a canal at Suez before it was actually built. When Napoleon Bonaparte was in Egypt, he ordered a survey made. His engineers figured that there was a difference of 29 feet between the levels of the Mediterranean and the Red seas, so Napoleon gave up the project.

It was not until 1854 that a French diplomat and engineer named Ferdinand de Lesseps was able to organize the construction of the canal. De Lesseps was on friendly terms with Said Pasha, the head of the Egyptian government. Said Pasha gave De Lesseps a concession to build the canal and to operate it for 99 years after the date of its opening. After that, it was to pass into the hands of the Egyptians.

De Lesseps organized a company to build the canal and sold shares in the company to raise money for the project. The greatest num-

Ferdinand de Lesseps, a French diplomat and engineer, organized the company that built the Suez Canal.

ber of shares were bought by Frenchmen. The Turkish Ottoman Empire acquired some, and the remaining shares were taken over by Said Pasha of Egypt.

The British bought no shares at this time and were opposed to the whole idea of the canal. They were afraid that it would mean French interference in their eastern colonies. Later, however—when Said Pasha was succeeded by Ismail Pasha—Benjamin Disraeli,

Travel through the Suez Canal shortens voyages by thousands of miles.

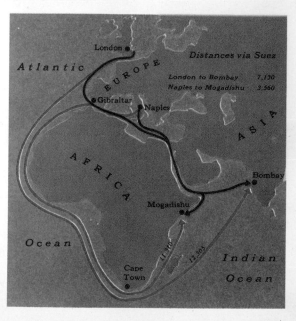

Four fifths of the men who worked on the Suez Canal were Egyptians. It took 10 years to build.

England's prime minister, persuaded Queen Victoria's government to buy the Egyptian shares in the canal.

Work on the canal started in April, 1859. By agreement with the Egyptian government four fifths of the workers were Egyptians. It took 10 years to build the canal, and De Lesseps encountered many difficulties. Finally, in November, 1869, the canal was formally opened. Sixty-eight ships of various nationalities started through the canal on November 17. They were led by the *Aigle*, a French ship, which carried the French Empress Eugenie. Halfway through the canal, at Ismaila, the ships stopped so that the passengers could attend inaugural celebrations. They did not continue on their way until November 19, and they reached Suez on November 20.

The canal was operated by De Lessep's company, with the French and English working together, for 40 years. In 1909, the Suez Company asked the Egyptian government to extend their lease on the canal. The lease was due to lapse in 1968. Their request was refused by the Egyptian parliament. During World War I, however, Egypt handed over the defense of the canal to the British military authorities. British and French forces patrolled the canal and closed it to any but Allied ships.

In 1950, during the Arab-Israeli war, Egypt refused to allow Israeli ships to pass through the Suez Canal. Later, in 1956, Egyptian President Gamal Abdul Nasser, who had been unable to raise funds for building the High Aswan Dam on the Nile river, seized the canal for Egypt. He announced that the tolls paid by shipping would be used to finance the dam. His act was protested by some of the European countries, and in October, Israel, Great Britain, and France attacked Egypt to regain control of the canal. The United Nations intervened at this point and sent troops to keep peace. In March, 1957, the canal was reopened by the Egyptian government, which now controls its operations. In 1959 the United Arab Republic secured a loan from the World Bank for the widening, deepening, and general improvement of the canal and Port Said.

Francisco Goya

Goya painted several self portraits, including this one in the Prado, Madrid.

Don Manuel Osorio de Zuñiga, *painted in 1788.*
Metropolitan Museum of Art, New York

When Francisco Goya painted a picture of the Spanish royal family, he made no effort to be flattering. The king, Charles IV, is red faced, determined, and bedecked with glittering medals. Queen Maria Luisa is arrogant and ugly. And the children, looking blank and foolish, are gaudily dressed. A French writer, seeing this picture, said that the people in it looked like "the grocer's family who have won the big lottery prize."

The strange thing was that the royal family liked the picture. They liked all of Goya's work, even when it insulted the nobility, the church, or the foolish conventions of the court.

Goya lived in a violent period of European history. In his native Spain, those who criticized the church or the crown were apt to be tortured to death. But Goya himself was so strong and robust a character and so great a painter of the life and people of his times that he lived his long life unharmed. He was honored by everyone.

Goya's full name was Francisco José de Goya y Lucientes. He was born of a peasant family in northern Spain in 1746. His talent for drawing soon became apparent. At 12 he painted a curtain for the altar in his village church. At 14 he was sent to the town of Saragossa to study under an artist named José Luzan Martinez. While he was there he became the friend of another painter, Francisco Bayeu, whose sister he later married.

The young Goya divided his time between painting and enjoying life. He liked to sing, to drink, and to fight, and he knew how to use a sword. He loved—and continued to love all his life—the people of the streets, gypsies, dancing girls, bullfighters, and young rowdies. And it was because he was involved in a brawl between two groups of young boys that Goya was forced to leave Saragossa. He fled to Madrid when he was 19, and there he mixed happily with the same kind of people. Another fight in Madrid left Goya in a gutter with a knife in his

The Bullfight *is part of Goya's bullfighting series. He was friendly with many bullfighters in Italy and* Spain.

Metropolitan Museum of Art, New York

WOLFE FUND, 1900

Goya painted many pictures of the Spanish royal family, including The Family of Charles IV *in 1800. Charles was Goya's protector during troubled years in Spain.*

Prado, Madrid

KODACHROME BY FRANCIS G. MAYER, NEW YORK CITY

The Maja Clothed (*left*), *painted about 1804. Prado, Madrid*

The Shooting of May Third, 1808, in Madrid (*on facing page*) *is one of Goya's oil paintings from 1814. Prado, Madrid*

back. Some friendly bullfighters took him out of the city and to Rome. He led the same kind of riotous life in Italy, but after two years there, he returned to Spain to take up painting again. At 29 Goya married Bayeu's sister. They moved to Madrid. Here he received a commission to design a series of tapestries for the royal family. These designs, or cartoons, as they were called, were not based on Greek classics as was usual in those days. Instead, they showed realistic scenes of everyday life in Spanish streets, villages, and farms. They were acclaimed, and almost immediately Goya and his work were in great demand. At 40 he became President of the Royal Academy of Fine Arts, and when Charles IV was made king, Goya became court painter. Charles IV was foolish and a tyrant, and he was dominated by his wife, Queen Maria Luisa. Goya had nothing but scorn for the royal family and the court. He often offended them, but they always forgave him. After one scandal, Goya was exiled to the country, but the king could not do without him, and he was soon recalled.

Goya did a series of etchings about this time called *The Caprices*, which made fun of everything from the courtiers to the army and the clergy. The etchings were so savagely critical that the Spanish church wanted to question him. But King Charles protected Goya by taking over the plates of the etchings and saying that they had been made at his order.

It was at this time that Goya, who was painting portraits of the most important people in Spain, painted the group picture of the royal family. Although his portraits were unflatteringly realistic, they were so human that people were pleased with them.

While Goya was at the height of his success, the French Revolution broke out. King Charles opposed the revolution, but later tried to come to terms with Napoleon when he invaded Spain. However, Napoleon forced Charles to abdicate, and his son Ferdinand VII became king. Napoleon then forced Ferdinand also to abdicate because he wanted to make his brother Joseph king of Spain. But the Spanish people fought the invaders everywhere in large and small struggles. The patriots who attacked the French forces in small groups became known as guerrilla—small war—fighters.

Goya's sympathies were with the French Revolution and the Bonapartes. But during this period, deeply moved by the plight of his own people, he painted the French slaughter of the Spanish at the gates of Madrid. This painting's vividness has reminded people ever since of the grimness of war. A series of etchings Goya made later, called the *Disasters of War*, shows the sufferings of civilians—starving women, dying babies, and men being shot by firing squads. Few artists have made the horror of war so real.

After Napoleon was driven out of Spain and conquered in Europe, Charles IV's son, Ferdinand VII, came back to the Spanish throne. He attacked everyone who had opposed him. Hundreds of Spaniards were killed, put to torture, or imprisoned by the new king. Goya was not threatened, but at 78 he could no longer tolerate life in his beloved Spain. He traveled to France, where he settled down to spend his last years in Bordeaux. There, surrounded by other Spanish refugees, he continued to paint, broadly, boldly, often wildly, using every instrument that came to hand. He died in Bordeaux at the age of 83 and was buried there. Some time later, his remains were brought back to Spain.

It has been said that Goya was as much a guerrilla fighter as the Spanish peasants he pictured so realistically. Certainly nothing in the troublesome era in which he lived ever caused him to be afraid. And nothing ever stopped him from painting the subjects he wanted to paint in the way he saw them.

Internal Combustion Engines

Water boiled in a pot turns to steam. Steam, trying to escape from the pot, will force the lid up. The heat of the fire has thus moved the lid. Heat has been turned into work.

The ancient Greeks knew that steam under pressure could be used to turn wheels and open doors, but no practical steam engines were invented until the 18th century. A steam engine is known as an external combustion engine because the combustion, or heating, takes place

bustion engines are among the most widely used sources of power in the world today.

THE GASOLINE ENGINE

The most common internal combustion engines are diesel engines and gasoline engines. The gasoline engine burns a mixture of air and gasoline inside a cylinder. The bottom of the cylinder is formed by a piston, which is forced down by the pressure of combustion. The com-

When water is boiled in a pot, heat is turned into work.

in the boiler *outside* the engine's cylinder. In other types of engines, the conversion of heat into work takes place *inside* the cylinder. These engines are known as internal combustion engines. Because of their comparative cheapness, convenience, and light weight, internal com-

bustion is actually a controlled explosion and drives the piston with considerable force. The internal combustion engine used in automobiles and airplanes is of the four-stroke cycle type and works in the following way:

First stage—the intake stroke: The piston

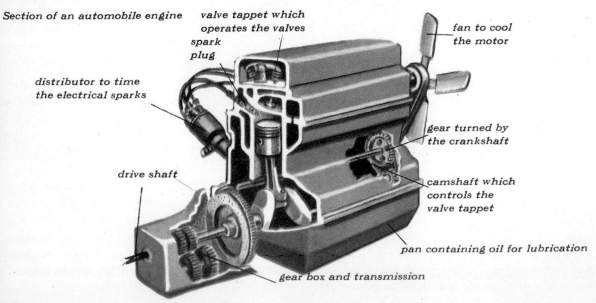

Section of an automobile engine
valve tappet which operates the valves
spark plug
fan to cool the motor
distributor to time the electrical sparks
gear turned by the crankshaft
drive shaft
camshaft which controls the valve tappet
pan containing oil for lubrication
gear box and transmission

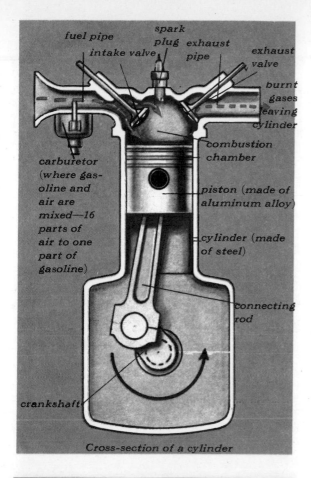

fuel pipe
spark plug
intake valve
exhaust pipe
exhaust valve
burnt gases leaving cylinder
carburetor (where gasoline and air are mixed—16 parts of air to one part of gasoline)
combustion chamber
piston (made of aluminum alloy)
cylinder (made of steel)
connecting rod
crankshaft

Cross-section of a cylinder

How a four-stroke cycle engine works

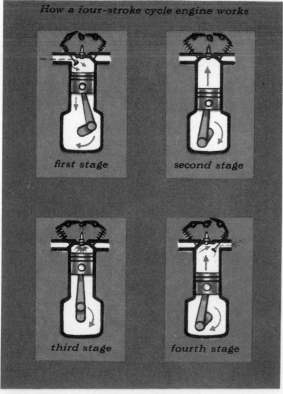

first stage

second stage

third stage

fourth stage

is pushed down in the cylinder. The intake valve on the left is opened automatically by the engine, and a mixture of air and gasoline is sucked into the cylinder. The mixture enters the cylinder as a mist of gasoline, which, when ignited, burns quickly and easily.

Second stage—the compression stroke: The piston, having come to the end of its downward stroke, is pushed to the top of the cylinder by the crank to which it is connected. The intake valve is now closed, and the fuel mixture in the cylinder is greatly compressed.

Third stage—the expansion or power stroke: As the piston reaches the top of its stroke, the compressed mixture of air and gasoline is ignited by a spark from the spark plug. The fuel burns very rapidly, creating gases at high temperature and pressure. The expansion of these gases forces the piston down in the cylinder. A connecting rod transmits the motion of the piston to the crankshaft, causing it to rotate. The crankshaft, through a drive shaft, drives the wheels of the car.

Fourth stage—the exhaust stroke: At the end of the power stroke the piston is at the bottom of the cylinder. As the connecting rod forces the piston back to the top of its stroke, the exhaust valve on the right opens, and the gases produced by the explosion are expelled from the cylinder, much as air is forced out of a bicycle pump. At the top of the stroke the exhaust valve closes, the intake valve opens, and the piston is ready to descend again for the intake stroke. The cycle is complete.

Only one out of these four strokes is the power stroke. The power for the other three strokes must come from somewhere. To compress a gas to a seventh of its bulk requires a fair amount of work, as pumping up a football will show.

There are two ways of providing the necessary power. Usually, an internal combustion engine consists of four or more cylinders, timed in such a way that one piston is always in its power stroke. This power stroke drives the crankshaft, which—by way of the connecting rods—drives the other three pistons through their intake, compression, and exhaust strokes. Thus, when the power stroke takes place in the

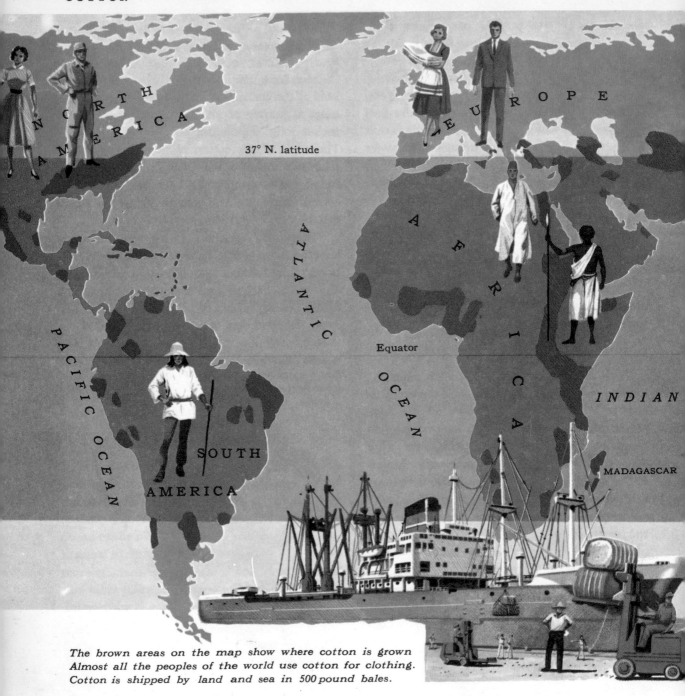

The brown areas on the map show where cotton is grown Almost all the peoples of the world use cotton for clothing. Cotton is shipped by land and sea in 500 pound bales.

the world's cotton is of the upland type. The fiber of upland cotton is coarser than that of sea-island cotton. It is three quarters of an inch to one and a quarter inches long. This is the type of cotton raised in the United States.

Cotton grows in the warm regions of the earth. It needs high temperatures, a lot of sunshine, and very fertile soil. Cotton needs

rain during the growing period, but when the boll opens and the cotton comes out, even a little wetting will ruin the fiber.

Although the cotton plant probably came originally from rainy tropical areas, man has moved it into the warm parts of the temperate zones. Here there is a lot of sun, but not too much rain. During droughts the crop can

ASIA

PACIFIC OCEAN

OCEAN

INDONESIA

AUSTRALIA

30° S. latitude

States leads the world in cotton production. The cotton-growing area of the United States is about 700 miles long and 2,000 miles wide. It includes most of the southern and southwestern states. In 1958 the United States produced almost 11,600,000 bales of cotton, 53 percent of the world's supply.

The biggest enemies of cotton are insect pests and diseases. The amount of United States cotton destroyed by insects in 1950 was valued at 900,000,000 dollars. The worst cotton pests are boll weevils, bollworms, red spiders, cutworms, and flea hoppers. Boll weevils are the most destructive of the pests. They came into Texas from Mexico in 1892 and have caused great damage to the cotton crop every year since that time. The female boll weevil lays her eggs in the cotton bud, which prevents it from maturing. The eggs need only 15 to 20 days to hatch and grow into adult boll weevils. These can then lay more eggs. The United States is constantly experimenting with new methods for getting rid of these pests.

Before 1794 it took one person a full day to clean a pound of cotton—to separate the fluff from the seed. In 1794 Eli Whitney invented the cotton gin. This machine pulled the cotton through iron grids, separating the seeds from the fibers. The invention of the cotton gin greatly increased the production of cotton. All gins now used are based on Whitney's invention.

No one knows how old the use of cotton may be, but it was a valuable material to man even in ancient times. Cotton is important today for many reasons. It can be used with little processing. It needs only to be cleaned. Even in countries of the world where spinning and weaving are not advanced, cotton is still the easiest fiber to work into cloth. It can be made into kinds of cloth so different from one another that it is hard to believe they all come from the same fiber. Organdy, so thin it is possible to see through it, is very different from the heavy canvas used for tarpaulins. Stiff crinoline for petticoats is unlike heavy, warm flannel. Velveteen and denim are not at all alike.

be irrigated. Most of the cotton in the world is grown in a belt about 4,500 miles wide, extending from 37 degrees north latitude to 30 degrees south latitude. It includes parts of the United States, South America, Africa, the Soviet Union, China, and southern Europe.

Because of good soil, suitable climate, and scientific advances in farming, the United

In 1765, Patrick Henry, the orator of the American Revolution, rallied the Virginia House of Burgesses to adopt his resolutions condemning the British Stamp Act.

The Intolerable Acts

The English came to North America at the beginning of the 17th century, and for about 150 years relations between the mother country and her colonies were friendly. But in the 1760's the friendship began to break down. The American Revolution followed and, finally, the United States of America was created.

Trouble began over taxes. The Seven Years' War in Europe, called the French and Indian War in the colonies, had been costly to the British. They decided the American colonies should help pay for the British military establishment that guarded them. In 1764 taxes were imposed on the importation of molasses, sugar, textiles, coffee, and other goods, and Parliament passed laws restricting trade.

The colonies objected. They had no representatives in Parliament, and they said that "taxation without representation is tyranny." Boston merchants agreed to do without lace and ruffles from England. By the end of the year the policy of not importing certain British goods had spread to other colonies.

In 1765 Parliament passed the Stamp Act. This was the first direct tax ever levied on the colonies by Parliament. The act placed a tax on newspapers, legal documents, insurance policies, licenses, and other such items—even on dice and playing cards. The colonists objected even more strongly than before. Patrick Henry, in the Virginia House of Burgesses, said that King George III of England should remember the fate of Charles I and Julius Caesar. Both of them were killed because they were tyrants. A Stamp Act Congress was held, and the colonies agreed not to import any goods at all from England.

As a result, the Stamp Act was repealed by the English government in 1766. But the colonists had only won a battle, not the war. In

1767 Parliament passed the Townshend Acts, which levied even heavier taxes on colonial businesses. The Americans objected again, especially the merchants of Massachusetts, and the next year England sent troops to Boston to keep order. This did not solve the problem. The presence of troops kept the spirit of rebellion alive, and in 1770 several Bostonians were killed by British soldiers in what came to be known as the Boston Massacre. But worse was still to come. From the Boston Massacre to the Battle of Bunker Hill to the Revolution itself were easy steps, for the English continued to levy taxes that the colonists thought restrictive and unfair.

One of the most famous incidents that helped to bring about the War of Independence occurred in 1773. It was not a question of taxation, but the colonists reacted to it as they had to Parliament's tax policy. The East India Company was on the verge of bankruptcy, and to save it from ruin, Parliament decreed that it could sell its tea in the colonies without having to pay the regular duties. This would have hurt American merchants, who had large stocks of tea on which they had paid duty. The East India Company would be able to undersell them, and the Americans were afraid a tea monopoly would be established, with headquarters in England.

The Boston Tea Party, in 1773, was an organized action of protest, led by Samuel Adams, against the British Tea Act. The colonists boarded the ships during the night and threw the tea overboard.

Mass meetings in the colonies condemned the Tea Act in late 1773. The *Dartmouth*, the first of three ships laden with tea, arrived in Boston harbor on November 27. The Bostonians refused to unload the ships. On the evening of December 16, about 8,000 people met in and near Boston's Old South Church. The captain of the *Dartmouth* told Samuel Adams, chairman of the meeting, that the British authorities would not yield. Massachusetts' Governor Thomas Hutchinson refused to give the ships permits to return to England until their cargoes of tea were unloaded. At a signal from Adams, a disciplined group of men, thinly disguised as Mohawk Indians, rushed to Griffin's Wharf, boarded the tea ships, and worked through the night dumping chests of tea into the harbor. No other property was touched, but 342 chests of tea were destroyed. This was known as the Boston Tea Party. As Sam Adams and his patriot followers had hoped, it rallied the other colonies behind the Bostonians in their struggle against British authority.

There were more tea disorders the next year. On April 22, 1774, members of the Sons of Liberty, an organization of leading New York merchants, dumped a cargo of tea into New York harbor. A tea cargo brought into Annapolis, Maryland, was burned on October 14.

The British Parliament met in March in an angry mood, determined to punish Massachusetts for having taken the leading role in the rebellious activities. The Boston Port Bill, which closed the port to trade, was passed. A Quartering Act legalized quartering of British troops in private homes in all the colonies. There were other repressive laws, which the colonists called the Intolerable Acts. Parliament also passed acts affecting western territories that angered colonists interested in the West.

By September 1, 1774, New England was preparing for war. In April, 1775, the battles of Lexington and Concord took place, and on May 10 Fort Ticonderoga was captured by the colonists. It was more than a year later that the colonies declared their independence of Great Britain, on July 4, 1776. But the Boston Tea Party and the events before and after it had made the declaration inevitable.

The Union of South Africa

The Union of South Africa covers the southern end of the African continent. It consists of four former British colonies, the Cape of Good Hope, Natal, Transvaal, and the Orange Free State. Within its boundaries are two British territories, Swaziland and Basutoland, which are governed by a British High Commissioner.

The Union of South Africa has two capitals. The administrative capital is at Pretoria, and the Parliament, consisting of an assembly and a senate, sits at Cape Town.

South Africa produces more gold and diamonds than any other country in the world. Recently uranium ore has been discovered there and a great quantity of uranium is now being produced by the Union. The country also has large amounts of coal, copper, tin, manganese, and other minerals.

South Africa is at the lower tip of Africa.

UNION OF SOUTH AFRICA
AREA: *472,494 square miles*
POP: *14,418,000*
CAPITAL: *Pretoria (Administrative), Cape Town (Legislative)*
RELIGIONS: *Dutch Protestant, Anglican, Methodist*
LANGUAGE: *Afrikaans, English*
MONETARY UNIT: *South African pound ($2.80)*

The climate of South Africa is mild and warm. Inland from the coast are high plateaus, or tablelands. Those in the southwest, which are dry and low, are called the karroos. In the east, the higher lands are known as the velds, which means grasslands. Only about six percent of the farm land is used for growing crops. Because there is little rain in most of South Africa, and there are only three important rivers, most of the land is more suitable for grazing cattle and sheep. The chief mountain range is the Drakensberg, which runs along the east and south of the tablelands.

Only one fifth of the people in South Africa are of white descent. Most of these are Dutch, known as Afrikanders, or English. The greater part of the population is called Natives by the whites. They are mostly Negroes of various Bantu tribes. There are a few of the original Bushmen and Hottentots in South Africa, but a great many of them have died out. Another group is called the Colored. They are part Negro and part white, a result of intermarriage between the earlier settlers and the Hottentots. There are also some Malays and Asiatics whose ancestors were brought to the country as slaves or servants during its early history.

Three fifths of the South African population lives in farm areas. Some 3,500,000 Natives live on government reservations in villages known as kraals—groups of round, domed huts built of straw or sod. Other Natives work for white farmers, or in the cities or mines.

Portuguese explorers looking for a route to India touched on the coast of South Africa during the 15th century. But the first settlement came two centuries later after some Dutch sailors, shipwrecked near the Cape of Good Hope in 1647, brought back praise of that country. In 1652 the Dutch East India Company sent a group of settlers to start a colony there. They were joined in 1687 by a group of French Huguenots. By about 1720 these colonists began to move inland. They had been on friendly terms with the Hottentots, who lived on the coast, but in the heart of the country they met Bantu tribesmen, who had come down from central Africa. The Bantu tribes resented the newcomers, and the struggle between them and the settlers continued for many years.

In 1795, during the Napoleonic wars, Britain seized South Africa to protect her sea route to India from Dutch interference. For a number of years Britain's claim to the country was negotiated and finally, in 1814, Holland sold the colony to Britain. At that time there were some 27,000 Dutch settlers in South Africa. They were known as Boers, the Dutch word for farmer.

In 1820 Britain sent 5,000 of her own settlers to the colony. The Boers resented the new arrivals, and between 1835 and 1843 some 12,000 Boers set out on what is known as the Great Trek. They moved north across the Orange River to found the Orange Free State, and across the Vaal River to form the Transvaal State. Britain acknowledged these states as an independent African republic in 1854.

In 1870, however, the Kimberley diamond fields were discovered in the Orange Free State, and a number of years later gold was discovered in the Witwatersrand near Johannesburg in the Transvaal. These discoveries started a great gold rush among the British and other

Sheep are important, and many Zulus are shepherds.

THE UNION OF SOUTH AFRICA

Europeans, who were referred to by the Boers as Uitlanders, or foreigners.

Cecil Rhodes, an Englishman who had made a fortune at the Kimberley diamond fields, became South Africa's prime minister. He dreamed of expanding British rule over Bechuanaland and Southern Rhodesia, both of which surrounded the Boer states. At the same

incorporate the territory into its own government. Although the U.N. refused the request, representatives of South-West Africa now take part in the Union Parliament, which makes the territory virtually part of South Africa.

To preserve the power and privilege of the white people, who are outnumbered four to one by the Natives and Coloreds, the government

Zulu—one of the Bantu peoples

European—of English or Dutch descent

Colored—people of mixed race

Bushman—one of the original natives

time, the president of Transvaal, Paul Kruger, organized a movement directed against the English Uitlanders. These disputes led to two wars between the Boers and the English. The British won the second Boer war—1899-1902. Their victory resulted in the establishment of the Union of South Africa in 1910. During World War I, South African troops defeated the Germans in South-West Africa, which was then German. In 1920 that section was mandated to the Union by the League of Nations, and it is now supposedly under U.N. protection.

Recently, however, the Union refused to turn South-West Africa over to a United Nations trusteeship. Instead, the Union wants to

has developed a policy known as Apartheid. Its purpose is to control the Negroes and to keep them from revolting against the government. Under Apartheid there is a strict separation of the whites and non-whites. The natives who work in the cities may not live in the same sections as the whites. Their houses are usually flimsy shacks in slums on the outskirts of the city. At the mines they are often housed in barracks. Schooling for non-whites is separate and is not encouraged by the government. Education is compulsory only for white children. No non-white may vote in the general national elections, and only whites serve in the Parliament. There is a separate election in which the

In South Africa's cities, the greatest part of the population is the native Negro.

natives may vote for the men—always white—who will presumably represent them in the Assembly.

Since 1948 the Nationalist Party, which is supported mostly by the Afrikander population, has been in power. It was under this government that the Apartheid rules were developed. As desire for freedom began to sweep over all the native peoples of Africa, the South African government realized that revolt was a very real danger, and the Parliament set out to try to make an uprising impossible. Various laws have prohibited strikes among native workers, restricted their travel, required separate living sections, controlled their education, and limited the kind of work they may do. These segregation policies and the way they have been enforced by the white minority are strongly condemned by most of the countries of the world. In 1956 criticism of the Apartheid policy in the U.N. led South Africa to withdraw all but a token representative from the organization in protest.

In 1958 Hendrik Frensch Verwoerd, a Nationlist minister who is totally committed to Apartheid, was elected president. Under his leadership the Union voted in 1960 to become a republic within the British Commonwealth. In 1961, however, other British Commonwealth nations were so critical of Apartheid that the Union of South Africa angrily withdrew from that association. At the same time the U.N. voted 95 to one, with no abstentions, a censure of the continued racial policies of South Africa.

Early Dutch settlers found friendly Hottentots.

River Ports and Seaports

Ports and harbors are very important today, just as they were in the earliest days of history. Sailors have found sheltered harbors in which to tie up their ships and markets for the goods the ships have carried. Ports are usually centers of business and commerce, and so they are often large and important.

River port, built at the mouth of the river

Inland river port

Duisburg, Germany, is the most important port on the Rhine. Many tugs and barges pass through it.

There are two kinds of ports built by man—those on rivers and those on seacoasts. Very often, as in the case of New York and Baltimore, a port is both a river port and a seaport. The seaports can usually handle bigger ships, but some inland river ports handle enormous quantities of cargo.

RIVER PORTS

Men have always settled along riverbanks because of the water and the roadway a river provides. Docks, warehouses, and wharves have been built as the traffic on the river increased.

At one time many river ports served as inland seaports. This was possible as long as sea ships were small enough to travel on rivers. At the time of the Romans, for example, Paris,

A view of San Francisco on the Sacramento River

The river port of Cologne on the Rhine.

Some of the most important river ports of the world are shown on the map below.

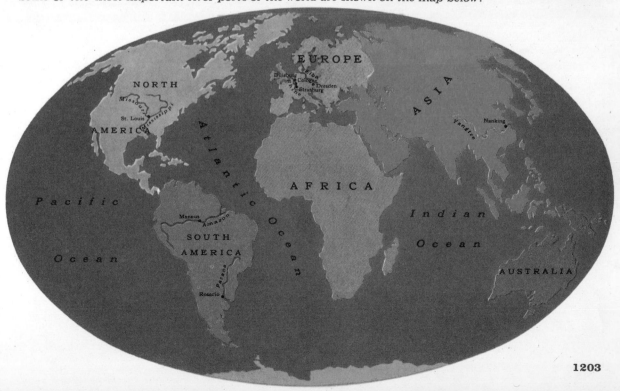

France, was an important port on the Seine River. Seagoing boats, as well as river barges, were moored along its quays. But as ships became larger, they could no longer follow the Seine to Paris. Then Rouen—also on the Seine, but nearer the sea—became the im-

The river port of St. Louis on the Mississippi

portant river port and remains a major French port today. The large transatlantic liners stop at Le Havre, the port at the mouth of the Seine. Only canal barges and ships of under 800 tons tie up along the quays of Paris today.

Other famous river ports are found along the Rhine—Strasburg, Duisburg, and Cologne are among the most important. Vessels of up to 4,000 tons can navigate as far as Cologne, and small steamships can reach the Swiss border, more than 400 miles from the sea. The Rhine passes through such heavily industrialized regions as the Ruhr, and connects with an excellent network of canals. Because of this, the river is important, and Duisburg has become one of the greatest inland river ports in the world.

Bollards are the iron posts fixed on docks to hold the lines of ships tied up in port.

Hartshorne anchor

Ships that cannot tie up at the docks must anchor in the harbor.

Hall anchor

Whistle buoy

Light buoys

Whistle and light buoys guide incoming ships to channels and away from navigation hazards.

St. Louis, on the Mississippi River, is one of the biggest ports in the United States. The Mississippi—with its main tributaries, the Missouri and Ohio—is to the United States what the Rhine is to Europe. Pittsburgh and Cincinnati on the Ohio, for example, are also important river ports and industrial centers. The city of Chicago, on the shores of Lake Michigan, has recently started a period of new activity as an inland port. The opening of the St. Lawrence Seaway in 1959 made it possible for ocean-going ships to reach such cities as Cleveland, Detroit, and Chicago. In time these cities—up to 1,000 miles inland—may become great seaports as well as great river ports.

SEAPORTS

River ports accommodate relatively small craft, such as barges and tugs, that dock there. But most rivers lead to the sea. And some of the greatest ports in the world—New York, Rotterdam, London—are at points where river ships meet ocean-going freighters, where goods are trans-shipped between small and large craft. Seaports are shelters that shield ships from ocean storms. Seaports provide fuel and repairs needed by ships that make voyages lasting for weeks or months. And it is in the seaports that the great merchant fleets of the world are built.

As the panorama shows, a seaport is a complicated and exciting place. Even before an ocean liner enters the harbor, it encounters the protection of the port. (See page 1204.)

The breakwater, or mole (1), is built of stone or concrete. It breaks the force of the seas and keeps the harbor waters calm even in a storm.

Beacons and lights (2) guide the ship day and night.

A small pilot boat (3) comes alongside the liner. The pilot of the small boat mounts to the bridge of the liner and guides the ship through the channel to its pier.

Powerful tugboats (4) guide the huge liners gently to their berths.

The inside of this model of a harbor can be divided into eight separate areas where different services are performed.

Section A is reserved for privately owned yachts, cabin cruisers, and other pleasure craft.

Section B is the part of the harbor used by commercial vessels. Here freighters load and unload their cargoes. Since it is important that ships make a rapid turn around in port, machines are used to speed their loading and unloading. Large mobile cranes (5), for example, hoist the goods on to the trucks or railroad cars. Warehouses are built near the docks for the storage of goods.

Section C is reserved for oil tankers. Special barriers (6) close off the water of this part of the harbor. This prevents spilled oil from spreading to other parts. There is always the danger that oil may catch fire. Pipelines and oil tanks (7) to transport and store oil are often found near the docks where the oil is delivered.

Section D is where ocean-going ships are repaired and overhauled. When its hull needs painting or repairs, a ship is put in dry dock (8). When it is in dry dock, the watertight doors are closed, and the water is pumped out. The hull is then left exposed, with the ship resting on keel blocks where it is supported by framing.

Section E is for ships that carry coal. Grab buckets and elevator transports (9) pick up the coal and deposit it directly in the waiting railroad cars.

Section F is where the ships that carry grain and cereals unload. Powerful suction pumps (10) suck the grain from the ship's hold and store it in the silos on the dock (11).

Section G is the quarantine station where passengers and seamen must be examined if there is any danger that they have a contagious disease, such as smallpox. Occasionally passengers must stay here for days or weeks before they are allowed to enter the country. Animals, too, such as goats, monkeys, and cattle, must sometimes stay in quarantine.

Section H is for passenger liners. Here are the customs office and baggage sheds (12) where the passengers embark and disembark and where they meet their friends. For most travelers, this is the center of the port.

EGYPT
AREA: *386,198 square miles*
POP: *24,026,000*
CAPITAL: *Cairo*
RELIGIONS: *Moslem, Christian, Jewish*
LANGUAGE: *Arabic*
MONETARY UNIT: *Egyptian pound ($2.87)*

IRAN
AREA: *628,060 square miles*
POP: *20,149,000*
CAPITAL: *Teheran*
RELIGION: *Shia branch of Islam*
LANGUAGE: *Farsi (Persian)*
MONETARY UNIT: *Rial (1.3¢)*

IRAQ
AREA: *172,000 square miles*
POP: *6,590,000*
CAPITAL: *Baghdad*
RELIGIONS: *Moslem, Jewish, Christian*
LANGUAGE: *Arabic*
MONETARY UNIT: *Dinar ($2.80)*

ISRAEL
AREA: *7,593 square miles*
POP: *2,105,530*
CAPITAL: *Jerusalem*
LANGUAGE: *Hebrew*
RELIGION: *Jewish*
MONETARY UNIT: *Israeli pound (55.6¢)*

JORDAN
AREA: *37,500 square miles*
POP: *1,636,000*
CAPITAL: *Amman*
RELIGIONS: *Moslem, Christian*
LANGUAGE: *Arabic*
MONETARY UNIT: *Jordan Dinar ($2.80)*

LEBANON
AREA: *4,000 square miles*
POP: *1,550,000*
CAPITAL: *Beirut*
RELIGIONS: *Christian, Moslem*
LANGUAGE: *Arabic*
MONETARY UNIT: *Lebanese pound (31.8¢)*

SAUDI ARABIA
AREA: *870,000 square miles*
POP: *6,500,000*
CAPITAL: *Riyadh*
RELIGION: *Moslem*
LANGUAGE: *Arabic*
MONETARY UNIT: *Riyal (22.2¢)*

SYRIA
AREA: *72,234 square miles*
POP: *4,267,000*
CAPITAL: *Damascus*
RELIGIONS: *Sunni Moslem, Christian*
LANGUAGE: *Arabic*
MONETARY UNIT: *Syrian pound (28¢)*

TURKEY
AREA: *296,500 square miles*
POP: *26,880,000*
CAPITAL: *Ankara*
RELIGION: *Moslem*
LANGUAGE: *Turkish*
MONETARY UNIT: *Lira (11.11¢)*

YEMEN
AREA: *75,000 square miles*
POP: *5,000,000*
CAPITALS: *Sana, Taiz*
RELIGIONS: *Shi'i, Islam, Shafi'is*
LANGUAGE: *Arabic*
MONETARY UNIT: *Silver riyal (80¢)*

The Near East

The Near East is the name given to a group of countries that lie at the eastern end of the Mediterranean Sea. Although Near East is not a very exact term, it is usually understood to include Egypt, Iran, Iraq, Israel, Jordan, Lebanon, Saudi Arabia, Syria, Turkey, and Yemen. In addition, certain areas on the fringes of the Arabian Peninsula which are not independent countries are part of the Near East. These are Aden Protectorate, the adjoining British Crown Colony of Aden, Kuwait, the Sheikdom of Qatar, the Sheikdom of Bahrein, the Trucial Sheikdoms, and the Sultanate of Muscat and Oman.

Two thirds of all the oil that is known to exist in the world is in the Near East. Some of the countries, such as Iran, Iraq, Saudi Arabia, and the Sheikdom of Kuwait, seem almost to float on great seas of this natural resource, which is so valuable that it is often called black gold.

Above ground, however, the Near East is one of the most desperately poor areas of the whole world. Because of lack of water, only about five percent of the land can be cultivated.

In most Near Eastern countries, there has been little change in the average person's standard of living for hundreds of years. Notable exceptions to this are Israel, a thoroughly modern country which was established as a nation by the United Nations in 1948, and Turkey, which has made considerable improvement in the way its people live in the last 40 years.

Although Near Eastern oil is now extremely important, not only to the countries involved but also to the West, the discovery of oil in that region is quite recent. In 1909, British engineers in Persia — which later became Iran — struck oil and founded the Anglo-Persian Oil Company. It wasn't until the early 1930's that Americans became involved in Near Eastern oil. At that time, Ibn Saud, the king of Saudi Arabia, allowed Americans to explore his country for oil. When oil was found, he gave concessions to companies that formed the Arabian American Oil Company, or Aramco. In exchange for the rights to produce oil, Aramco pays royalties to

Saudi Arabia for each barrel of oil that is produced. In general, all foreign companies producing oil in the Near East pay such royalties. The oil business, therefore, is a tremendously important source of income to the Near East.

Even in some countries where little oil has been found, the petroleum industry can be a great source of income to the government. For example, Syria has few oilfields of its own. But Syria allows Iraq and Saudi Arabia to run pipelines across its territory to the Mediterranean. For this, the Syrian government is paid transit fees by all users of the pipelines. Altogether, income from their vast oil fields has brought thousands of millions of dollars to Near Eastern governments in the last 20 years.

The Soviet Union does not own a single drop of Near Eastern oil. At the present time, it has enough oil for its needs within its own borders. Russia is interested in the Near East for other reasons, however.

For hundreds of years, Russia has wanted a warm-water port on the Mediterranean. A warm-water port is one that does not freeze up in the winter and from which shipping can be carried on easily all year round. The lack of such a port is so serious for Russia that this vast country has been described as "a mansion with a thousand windows but no gate." Control of the Dardanelles, the straits that connect the Black Sea with the Mediterranean, would give Russia the

entrance to the Mediterranean that she wants. But Turkey, which owns the straits, is a traditional enemy of the Russians and has refused repeatedly to give Russia any power in the Dardanelles. After World War II Russia again made a bid to get possession of these Black Sea straits, and again was unsuccessful. Russian merchant ships use the Dardanelles freely. It is only in the matter of control and defense of the straits that Russia is forbidden to take part.

Oil and ports are not the only reasons that the West and the Russians have been interested in the Near East. One of the earliest reasons for the world's concern with this sandy, desolate region was because of its geographical location. Lying as it does at the junction of the European, African, and Asian continents, the world's most important trade routes have always run through the Near East. Baghdad, Istanbul (Constantinople), and Damascus have been traditionally famous for the fabulous goods from all parts of the world that have appeared in their markets.

Although these old overland trade routes are no longer important, the Near East is still wooed by the Soviets for its ports and its access to Africa. The West wants not only to retain its oil rights, but to keep the Near East as a non-Communist buffer zone between the U.S.S.R. and Africa. In 1955, an organization was started, with Western blessing, to block Soviet moves into the Near East. The organization, at first

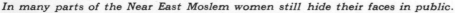

In many parts of the Near East Moslem women still hide their faces in public.

known as the Baghdad Pact, was later renamed the Central Treaty Organization.

The modern history of the Near East has been the story of its struggle for independence. Like people in other parts of the world, the Arabs have fought to establish their own free nations. Now, except for the small sheikdoms at the fringes of the Arabian peninsula, all the Near Eastern countries are independent.

This independence is recent. Throughout their early history, the countries of the Near East were conquered repeatedly—first by the Persians, then by the Greeks, next by the Romans, and later by the Byzantine Romans. As each empire collapsed, another took its place.

In the 13th century a Turkish leader named Othman set out to conquer the tribes and areas around him. He was the first of a family of rulers who established what became known as the Turkish Ottoman Empire. This empire controlled not only the Near East and Egypt, but parts of Asia Minor, North Africa, and the Balkans.

It was a powerful empire and, though its power gradually dwindled away, the empire lasted until after World War I. In that war, the Ottoman Empire sided with Germany against the Allies. The Empire was dissolved at the end of the war and the Arab countries that had been formerly ruled by it were placed under the mandate, or protection, of the British and the French. The British were given the mandates of Iraq, which was once called Mesopotamia, Palestine, which is now Israel, and Transjordan, which is now Jordan. The French received the mandates of Syria and Lebanon. Gradually all of these mandated countries gained their independence and joined the United Nations. They all became republics except Jordan, which is ruled by a king, and is therefore a monarchy.

One of the first of the Arab leaders to gain control in his own country was Ibn Saud of Saudi Arabia. Even before the fall of the Ottoman Empire, he had conquered most of the small sheikdoms on the Arabian peninsula, and was working to bring them together and to build up that poor and barren country. One of the ways he built it up was to sell oil rights to the United States.

Many men wear long, loose fitting garments, which help keep out the dry heat of the area.

Other nationalist revolutions took place in other parts of the Near East. In Egypt, Mohammed Naguib forced the tyrannical king to abdicate in 1952. In 1953 Egypt was declared a republic. Naguib was overthrown the following year by Gamal Abdul Nasser. Although Egypt is racially the least Arabic of all the Arab countries, Nasser then tried to create a United Arabia. In 1958 Syria merged with Egypt to form the United Arab Republic—two states, governed by one executive council. Nasser became the first president of this council. The third nation, Yemen, joined Nasser's United Arabia only in a limited way. Yemen insisted on keeping its own independent rule, but joined with the United Arab Republic to form still another group called the United Arab States.

The revolution that established Israel was another type of nationalist revolution. It took the Jews about 30 years of negotiation and fighting to get the British to give up their Palestine mandate. Finally in 1948, its boundaries having been established by the United Nations, Israel became an independent country. It immediately began a fight for its life. Jordan, Egypt, Lebanon, and Syria all attacked it. Israel beat off these attacks. To help keep the peace, a United Nations emergency force was formed for the first time in history, and sent to Israel to do police duty along that new country's borders.

Japanese houses are light and flexible so that they may withstand the shock of earthquakes.

An Eskimo's igloo is built of ice blocks.

Houses

Human beings need some form of shelter. What the shelter is built of, what it looks like, and how large it is depend on the materials that are available, the skill of the builders, and the needs of those who live in it.

In crowded cities apartment houses of many stories are built so that more people can fit into one building. In the southwestern part of the United States houses are built of adobe clay because the clay is abundant, and the thick adobe walls keep the inside of the house cool during the hot summer.

The Eskimo builds a temporary house out of what he has the most of—ice. He piles blocks of ice in smaller and smaller circles to make a dome-shaped igloo. He leaves an air hole at the top and another opening at the side which serves as a door.

A Japanese house is another example of how a building depends upon the materials at hand. Wood is plentiful in Japan, so it is used instead of brick or stone as the main building material. From rice, which is grown in Japan, a paper called rice paper is made. Rice paper is often used in windows in place of glass and for indoor partitions. It lets in light, but it is not transparent.

Primitive men knew that they needed a place to live in order to protect their families from bad weather and wild animals. They made their homes in caves. Later they started to build on to their caves. They put up a wall of rocks a few feet in front of the cave and then built a roof of logs or skins to cover the space lying between the wall and the opening of the cave.

When man began to live in places where there were no natural caves, he had to build his entire house. The simplest house to build was a hut made of branches, grass, and mud. Some huts were built on the ground. Others were built in trees or on stilts over the water as protection from animals. Today primitive peoples in many parts of the world still live in this kind of house.

At first the huts had only one room. Eventually this one room was divided into two or more smaller rooms. In Europe thousands of years ago people began to put several of these huts together on one platform. At about the same time men began to use crossed logs for their houses. These houses looked much like the log cabins built by American frontiersmen.

The first brick houses were built in ancient Egypt. They had wooden ceilings and brick walls which were often painted. Some of them were two or more stories high. They were built according to one of two different floor plans.

Some African people build round, one-room huts, called rondhovels.

The Stone Age platform house was built of crossed logs and had a thatched roof.

A copy of an early Egyptian brick house

Roman houses were built around central courtyards called atria.

An Arabian house is richly decorated.

The first plan was called a block house. Except that it was built of brick instead of logs and grass, it was similar to the platform house of prehistoric times. The second plan included a courtyard. Usually the court was enclosed by walls on two sides and the L-shaped house on the other two sides.

The Etruscans of northern Italy, and later the Romans, also built their houses around a central court. Their houses were built of clay brick, and the walls between the rooms were made of wood. Houses of clay brick with central courtyards are still being built in many of the Arab countries, but they are more richly decorated than the early Roman houses were.

The Medieval castle was designed so that it could be defended from enemies.

For many centuries there were few changes in the materials used for building. During the Middle Ages, stone, brick, and wood were still the usual materials. Glass was used for some of the windows, which were usually very tiny. But important changes were made in house plans during this time. Villages became busier, and more people moved into towns, so houses had to take up less room.

The city houses were long and narrow and two or three stories tall. Each floor had two rooms, one behind the other, separated by a small court. But there were no real hallways. On the first floor there was usually a shop in front and a kitchen in back. On the second floor, which could be reached by a spiral staircase, the front room was a living room and the back room a bedroom. The inside of the city house stayed about the same all through the 13th, 14th, and 15th centuries, but the outside was more richly decorated as time went on.

Medieval country houses did not undergo many changes. The nobles continued to live in castles. The workers lived in simple one or two room cottages with mud walls and thatched roofs. In France, during the 13th century, workers' cottages were built of stone instead of mud. In Germany, Switzerland, and Scandinavia working people lived in log houses called chalets. Many people in those areas still live in chalets because wood can be obtained easily and cheaply. The chalets are built of heavy logs which keep out the cold weather and are strong enough to support the deep snow that collects on the roofs.

The Scandinavian chalet is built of heavy logs.

During the late 15th century greater stress was placed on planning for convenience as well as for shelter. Rooms were separated by hallways for easier passage from one room to another, and the number of rooms was increased. People also wanted the designs to be as balanced as possible. Often houses were divided in half by a wide hall, with a room on each side. One half of the house was the mirror image of the other half. And if there was a stairway on one side of the hall, there had to be a matching stairway on the opposite side. This balanced house plan became very popular in 18th century England and was an important part of Georgian architecture. Such houses were also built in the United States at the same time. They were either of brick or of wood.

Toward the end of the 18th century the Industrial Revolution began. With the invention of machines and the building of factories, more people came to live and work in cities. They did not need workshops in their homes, so the city houses were smaller.

During the 19th century progress was also made in electricity and plumbing. One-family houses were centrally heated, and their kitchens were designed to save space, time, and work. They often had more than one bathroom.

Perhaps the most important development in building material occurred at the end of the 19th century when builders began using concrete and steel. One steel beam could do the work of a long thick wall in supporting a ceiling. And the outside walls could be curved without using specially cut brick or stone.

Steel and concrete also allowed much greater use of glass. Entire walls could be made of glass with only a few steel supports. Today this use of glass provides a kind of indoor-outdoor living that many people enjoy.

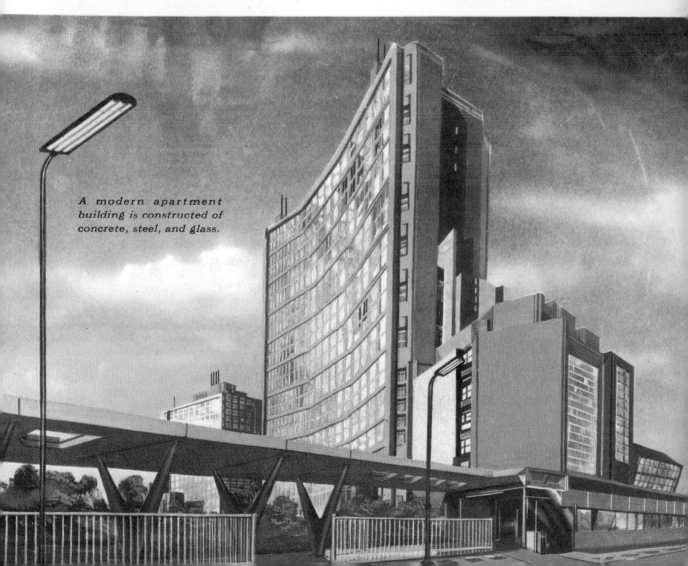

A modern apartment building is constructed of concrete, steel, and glass.

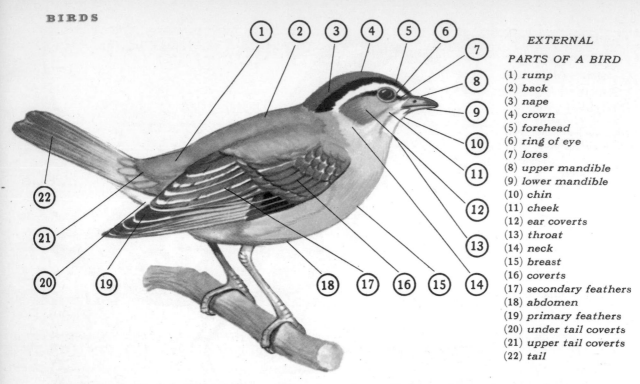

EXTERNAL
PARTS OF A BIRD
(1) *rump*
(2) *back*
(3) *nape*
(4) *crown*
(5) *forehead*
(6) *ring of eye*
(7) *lores*
(8) *upper mandible*
(9) *lower mandible*
(10) *chin*
(11) *cheek*
(12) *ear coverts*
(13) *throat*
(14) *neck*
(15) *breast*
(16) *coverts*
(17) *secondary feathers*
(18) *abdomen*
(19) *primary feathers*
(20) *under tail coverts*
(21) *upper tail coverts*
(22) *tail*

tains gravel and sand the bird has swallowed. As the gizzard contracts, the gravel and sand grind up the food.

The kind of food birds eat is as varied as the size and appearance of the birds themselves. Hummingbirds like nectar and suck it from flowers with their long, thin bills. Their wings beat with great speed as they hover in the air to feed. Geese are vegetarians and eat grass. The cuckoo prefers caterpillars, and the swallow likes small insects, which it can catch in midair. Some birds live on seeds, and their beaks are constructed for cracking them. Other birds, such as hawks and eagles, attack and devour small animals. A few eat carrion—animals that are already dead.

All female birds lay eggs. Before the eggs are to be laid, most birds begin to build nests.

Some birds, such as the ostrich, have nests that are common property, shared with other birds of the same species. Some, such as the cuckoo, lay their eggs in their neighbors' nests. But most birds prepare their own nests. The eggs take from 10 days to eight weeks to hatch. Usually the female sits on them to keep them warm until the chicks are ready to emerge, but sometimes the parents take turns. Until the young birds learn to fly, the parents spend most of their time caring for them. They feed, teach, and protect them until they are strong enough to leave the nest and take care of themselves.

In regions where winters are cold, many birds fly to warmer climates in the autumn. In the spring they return. They usually migrate in flocks and travel at night.

Arrangement of feathers in three phases of a wingbeat

descending   *about to be lifted*   *being lifted*

The Beginnings of Mankind

The 18th century Swedish scientist Karl von Linné, commonly known as Linnaeus, classified all living creatures into groups. He put monkeys, apes, and man into a group which he called primates, or first animals. He labeled man *Homo sapiens,* which means thinking man.

Since the 18th century, archeologists and anthropologists have traced much of the history of *Homo sapiens.* They have unearthed fossils and bones, which can be dated according to the layers of earth and rock in which they were found, as well as by the types of tools and implements found with them. In addition, there are chemical and physical tests for determining their age.

Scientists believe that the first forms of modern man appeared during the Pleistocene period, which began about 1,000,000 years ago. During the Pleistocene period great gla-

The remains of Peking man were found at Dragon Bone Hill, near Peking, China, in 1929.

ciers advanced and retreated in Europe, North America, and Asia. Each of these glaciers caused changes in the animal life of the continents. Studying and comparing these changes is another aid in dating the specimens of prehistoric man.

There are still many gaps in our knowledge of man's development. But discoveries in vari-

ous parts of the world have told us a good deal.

In 1891 a young Dutch army doctor, Eugene Dubois, made an important discovery in Java. He found the skull and thighbone of an apelike man who probably lived over 600,000 years ago. The shape of the thighbone showed that he walked upright, not on all fours like an ape. His skull was smaller than a modern

This map shows various parts of the world where remains have been found of Peking, Neanderthal, and Cro-Magnon man.

man's, but it had more brain capacity than an ape's. The jaw structure showed that he could make a few sounds, although not language as we understand it. He did not know how to build a fire, so he ate his meat raw. Dubois named this specimen *Pithecanthropus erectus*, from Greek words which mean apeman erect.

In 1903 a German scientist in Peking, China, found druggists selling pulverized fossilized bones as medicine. Among some unground fossils the scientist uncovered a human tooth, but he could not learn where it had been found.

In 1926 two more human teeth were found in a village near Peking. A spot there called Dragon Bone Hill was covered with caves that

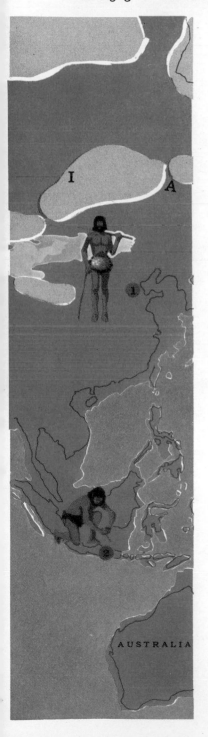

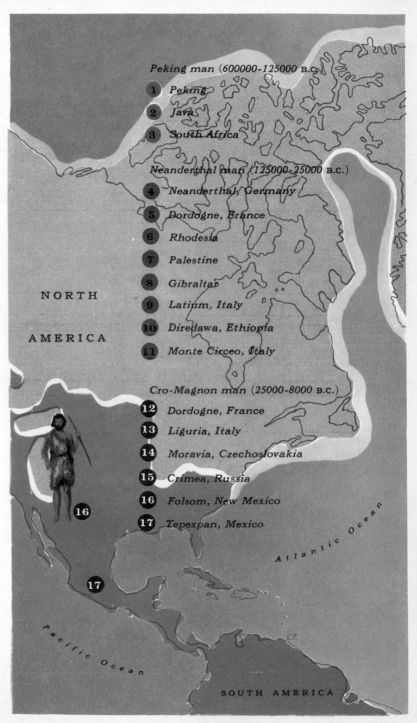

Peking man (600000-125000 B.C.)
1 Peking
2 Java
3 South Africa

Neanderthal man (125000-25000 B.C.)
4 Neanderthal, Germany
5 Dordogne, France
6 Rhodesia
7 Palestine
8 Gibraltar
9 Latium, Italy
10 Diredawa, Ethiopia
11 Monte Circeo, Italy

Cro-Magnon man (25000-8000 B.C.)
12 Dordogne, France
13 Liguria, Italy
14 Moravia, Czechoslovakia
15 Crimea, Russia
16 Folsom, New Mexico
17 Tepexpan, Mexico

had filled up over the years with dirt and pebbles. This had gradually hardened, and the scientists had to blast the hard earth and sift through all the rubble to find specimens.

In 1929 Dr. Davidson Black, a Canadian, led a group of scientists from many countries to explore Dragon Bone Hill. At the end of the year, when they were about to give up their digging for the winter, they made a tremendously important discovery. Dr. Pei, a Chinese archeologist in charge of the diggings at the time, uncovered an entire human skull embedded in a block of stone. This valuable discovery was later named the Peking man.

In later years the skeletal remains of about 40 men, women, and children were found in Dragon Bone Hill. They were somewhat more advanced than Java's Pithecanthropus man. They were more human than apelike, but they had apelike ridged foreheads and receding chins. Their brain capacity was about three fourths that of modern man, but far greater than that of the ape, which has less than half of man's brain capacity.

These ancient people had crudely shaped flints and primitive weapons made of deer antlers. They had hearths, which indicates that they knew how to make and use fire.

The next major stage in the development of man that has been uncovered is the Neanderthal stage. Bones of Neanderthal man were first found in 1856. A group of workmen digging at a place called Neanderthal, near Dusseldorf, Germany, found some arm and leg bones, the top of a skull, fragments of shoulder bones, and a pelvis. These bones were preserved and studied, and by 1858 scientists recognized them as belonging to a very early type of man. Since then, Neanderthal bones have been found in Belgium, Spain, Italy, Yugoslavia, France, Palestine, and North Africa.

Scientists believe that the primitive Neanderthals lived for about 70,000 years and that they became more highly developed during the latter part of their history.

Neanderthal man was usually not much more than five feet tall. He had a low forehead that sloped back like an ape's, but the ridge on

Peking man lived about 600,000 years ago. He knew how to make and to use fire.

Neanderthal man lived from 125,000 to 25,000 years ago. The first specimen was found in Germany.

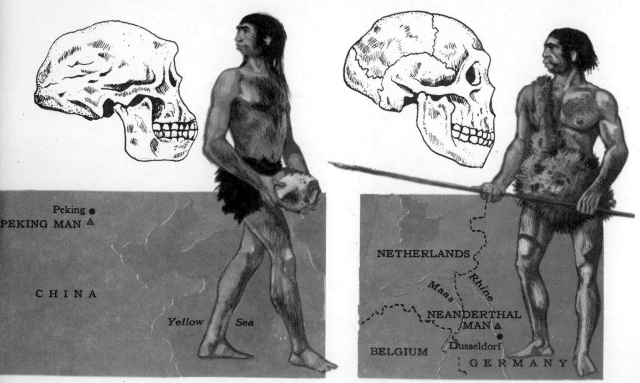

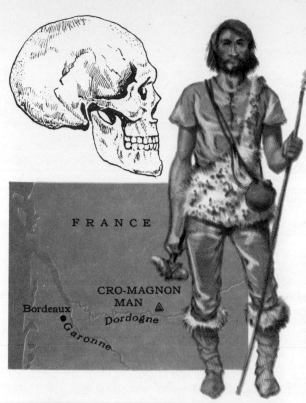

Cro-Magnon man probably lived between 25,000 and 10,000 years ago. He made fine stone tools, and pottery, and painted on the walls of caves.

neath the original find. Since then, Cro-Magnon skeletons have been found in many other parts of Europe. They were called Cro-Magnon from the dialect of the French workers who made the first find and referred to the cave as *cro magnon*, or great hole.

Cro-Magnon man lived in the last part of the Pleistocene period and looked very much like modern man. He was taller than Neanderthal man—sometimes as much as six feet tall. He had a high forehead and no heavy ridge across it. His cheekbones were wide, his nose and chin prominent.

From his tools and weapons we can tell that Cro-Magnon man led a different life from more primitive men. He had engraving tools for carving on stone. He used anvils and hammer stones. He had flint knives that were dull on one side and sharp on the other so that he could work without cutting his hand. He made needles and awls, so he probably sewed his clothing, although crudely. He liked ornaments. In Cro-Magnon graves scientists have found necklaces, bracelets, and anklets made of snail shells or stag's teeth, carved bone, and sometimes ivory.

Earlier Cro-Magnon man carved crude statuettes and etched pictures in the stone of caves. Later Cro-Magnon man used red clay or carbon from the fire and mixed these with animal fat to paint pictures on cave walls. The pictures show the animals of that day, animals that don't exist in southern Europe now. There are pictures of bison, mammoths, reindeer, prehistoric horses, and some unidentifiable animals. The pictures were probably painted to bring luck to hunters. They were not painted in the caves where the Cro-Magnons lived, but in special caves not used for dwellings. There are Cro-Magnon paintings, preserved in sealed caves for thousands of years, that appear vivid and real today, perhaps just as they were when they were painted.

Other important discoveries in the history of early man include Heidelberg man, from Heidelberg, Germany, Rhodesian man of Africa, and Solo man of Java. There is still a great deal that is not known about early man, but discoveries and study are continuing.

his forehead did not run all the way across as Peking man's did. Neanderthal man was heavily built and had a thick neck. He probably used only simple sounds to express himself. He knew how to make fire and tools. Because he buried his dead, archeologists have found many more skeletons of Neanderthal man than of earlier types. It is likely that Neanderthal man had some belief in afterlife, because he buried tools and weapons with the bodies. We know he wore animal skins, because tools for scraping and dressing furs have been found. No needles or awls have been found, so he probably did not know how to sew. He probably wore a single skin for warmth.

Another important group among primitive men is the Cro-Magnon. The first remains of Cro-Magnon man were found in 1868. Workers building a railroad in Les Eyzies, a French village, in the Dordogne Valley, came across some weapons and animal bones. Experts were called in, and they discovered two skulls and some bones in a cave. When they dug farther, they uncovered four other skeletons buried be-

Ancient India

In 1924 an archeologist named John Marshall described an astonishing discovery he had made. While digging at Mohenjo-Daro in Pakistan, which was then part of India, he uncovered the ruins of a city that was more than 5,000 years old.

The astonishing thing about the discovery was that no one at that time knew that any people capable of building such a city had existed in India 3,000 years before Christ or, in fact, for a thousand years after that. Another amazing feature discovered was that the ancient city at Mohenjo-Daro had had facilities that were unknown in parts of Europe as late as the 1800's.

Archeologists could tell from the ruins that the city had had wide streets lined with brick buildings and apartment houses. Each house had had its own tiled bathroom. Covered drains throughout the city had provided an efficient sewerage system. And there were community swimming pools.

Furthermore, archeologists could tell without a doubt that Mohenjo-Daro's people had systems of writing, counting, weighing, and measuring. It was obvious from the network of ditches and canals surrounding the city that they also had understood how to irrigate their farmland. Finely decorated gold and silver coins and ivory seals were found in the excavation, indicating that there had been artists as well as engineers and architects. From the perfectly shaped clay pitchers and bowls that were found, archeologists could be sure that these people had used a potter's wheel.

Unfortunately, very little is known about what happened to these early Indians. In fact, we know that they existed at all only because of the ruins of their remarkable city.

ARYANS AND DRAVIDIANS

Before the discovery of the ancient city at Mohenjo-Daro, Indian culture was thought to have begun about 4,000 years ago, when wandering bands of Aryans from Asia invaded India. *Aryan* is a Sanskrit word meaning nobleman or landowner. The Aryans, a fair-skinned and rather highly civilized people, found dark-skinned tribes living in India, among them the Dravidians. The Dravidians may have been the descendants of the people who built the city at Mohenjo-Daro 1,000 years earlier. They are

thought to have looked like the girl in the drawing below. Many of these native Indians fled before the Aryan invaders. In some remote parts of India their descendants still live primitive and remote lives. But some Dravidians stayed in northern India where the Aryans settled. There the Dravidians intermarried with the Aryan conquerors.

During the next 1,000 years, under the Aryan influence, the Sanskrit language was perfected by the people and a way of writing was devised. The caste system, which divided people into sharply separated classes, dates from this period, when the Aryans were conquering and dominating the more primitive people of India. The caste system still exists in Indian life today.

The people who built the city at Mohenjo-Daro may have looked like this Indian girl.

Above is a wood carving of Agni, the god of fire. Below is a statue of Brahma, the chief god of the Indians during the Vedic period.

AGNI AND BRAHMA

The sacred books of India, the Vedas, tell a great deal about how the ancient Indians lived. There were many Vedas written over a long period of time. Some are thought to have been written as early as 1000 B.C. Although the word *veda* means knowledge, the books are primarily religious. They contain the origins of the present Hindu faith. Agni, as shown in the top statue to the right, was one of the gods of the early Vedas. He was the god of fire and had two heads to represent the two kinds of fire he symbolized—the fire in the home and the sacrificial fire in which animals were sacrificed to the Vedic gods.

During the Vedic period, Brahma, shown in the statue to the right, gradually became the principal god of the Indians. He is usually shown in sculpture with four faces, supposedly so that he could keep watch over the universe in every direction at once. The priests who

worshiped Brahma were called Brahmani. The name Brahman, stemming from these early priests, is still the name given to the highest caste in Indian life.

ARCHITECTURE

As in most countries, the most imposing examples of early architecture in India are found in religious buildings. The Temple of Ellora, above, was built in the eighth century A.D. It was dedicated to the god Siva. The elephants that form the base of the temple were all carved out of a single mass of rock. This richly decorated temple is considered one of the architectural marvels of the world.

Another example of early Indian architecture is this fragment, at the right, found near Benares. It is a capital, or top of a pillar, used to hold up a roof.

One of India's most unusual temples is the pyramid-shaped structure at the far right, built in the sixth century A.D. at Gaya. It was built on the spot where Gautama Buddha was supposed to have first taught the principles of his new religion, Buddhism, hundreds of years earlier. Although most Indians are now Hindus rather than Buddhists, this interesting early temple is still carefully tended, and inside it lamps are constantly kept burning before a statue of Buddha.

Lions carved out of rock make the capital of a column that holds up the roof of an ancient building.

The temple above was part of three groups of temples built at Ellora— Hindu, Buddhist, and Jain.

Gaya, the site of the Buddhist temple at the right, is a Buddhist pilgrimage center.

Medieval Siege Weapons

The ancient Greeks and Romans developed many weapons for attacking cities and walled fortresses. But during the Dark Ages, when there was little communication among countries, knowledge about these machines was lost to the people of Europe. Only the Arabs, who traveled through a large part of the civilized world, learned and preserved the knowledge of the early weapons.

In the 11th century the Seljuk Turks took over the Holy Sepulchre, the tomb of Christ, and Pope Urban II asked the feudal lords of Europe to give up their private battles and join together in recapturing the city of Jerusalem. There were eight expeditions called the Crusades. The first one started in 1096.

Many of the Crusaders passed through Arab countries, and those men who returned brought

back much ancient knowledge that had not been able to penetrate the wall of ignorance that surrounded Europe. One of the skills they learned was the making of weapons that could be used to attack armed cities.

Scaling ladders (1) raised the soldiers to the tops of city towers. The penthouse (2) protected soldiers charging a fortress. The trebuchet (3) hurled boulders or burning material over the walls. Battering rams (4) would eventually make the heaviest gate give way.

The ballista (5) worked like a great bow to throw rocks or arrows at the enemy. Mantelets (6) were shields that were more easily moved than penthouses, but they protected only one or two soldiers. The assault tower (7) gave the fighters better protection than scaling ladders, but they were so huge that they were difficult to transport.

The Crusaders used these weapons in Jerusalem and later in Europe when they returned to fight their private wars again.

The Age of the Earth

The age of the earth and what has happened since its beginning have puzzled and intrigued men since early modern times. Although scientists agree that the earth is billions of years old, it is difficult to determine its exact age. To measure the earth's age, calculations are derived from geological studies. Geology is the science that deals with the structure, substance, and history of the earth.

One of the leading methods for determining the earth's age is stratigraphy, which deals with the age of sedimentary layers of rock and the order in which they have been deposited. Stratigraphy assumes that the lowest layer of rock in a series of layers is the oldest and that they decrease in age as they get closer to the surface.

Another method for determining the earth's age is radioactivity, which deals with the rate of chemical decay of mineral substances. Some elements and minerals decay in such a way that in an exact number of years half of their

Imprint of a reptile fish from the Mesozoic era

The glaciers of the Pleistocene period must have looked much like the Alaska glacier shown here

Fossils of ancient tree trunks have been found in the Arizona desert. These fossils are petrified— turned to stone—the molecules of the wood having been replaced by molecules of silicon.

Geologists reconstruct geological events by examining layers of sedimentary rock.

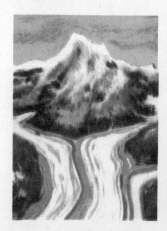

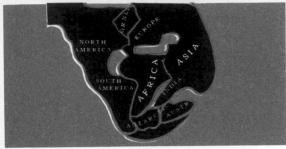

It is believed that early in the Archeozoic era the granite continents were joined together.

The probable distribution of the sea and land in the Devonian period of the Paleozoic era.

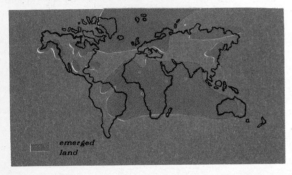

emerged
land

Distribution of the sea and the land in the Cretaceous period of the Mesozoic era, 200,000,000 years ago

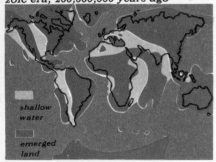

shallow
water

emerged
land

The probable distribution of the sea and land in the Pliocene period, about 90,000,000 years ago

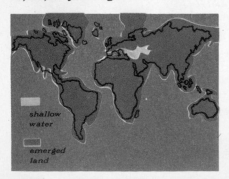

shallow
water

emerged
land

substance turns into lead or some other base element through radioactivity. This is called the half-life of the element or mineral. Using the half-life of such elements as thorium and certain kinds of carbon, scientists are able to determine the age of a specific rock by determining the amount of the radioactive element and of the base material.

By using stratigraphy and paleontology— the study of fossil remains of animals and plants that are found in sedimentary rocks— geologists can put together a picture of plant and animal life during the stages of the development of the earth's crust.

In geologic time, weeks, months, and years are insignificant. If we compared geologic history with a calendar year, life developed from worms and sponges after Thanksgiving. The last era occurred after Christmas, and man has lived in North America less than five minutes. Geologists use a time scale based on great changes in the earth's surface rather

Many of the land forms that still exist are the result of the action of glaciers. During the Pleistocene period ice covered northern Europe.

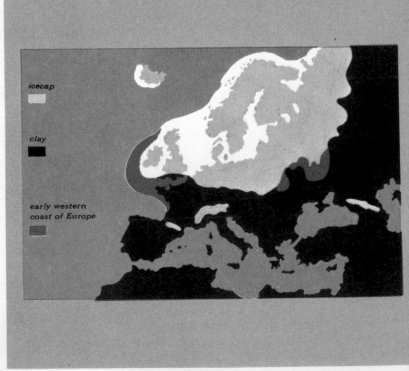

icecap

clay

early western
coast of Europe

An external mold of a giant ammonite, a mollusk that lived in the Mesozoic era. The animal was gradually covered by layers of soil. As these hardened, the animal and skeleton dissolved, leaving the form of the mollusk fixed in the rock.

than a specific number of years. Time differences are measured in millions of years and are approximate. The geologic time scale is broken down into eras. Eras are divided into periods, periods into epochs, and epochs into ages.

The dividing lines for eras are based on major crustal movements that effect most of the earth. The entire scale can be broken down into six eras—Asoic, Archeozoic, Proterozoic, Paleozoic, Mesozoic, and Cenozoic.

Knowledge of the first three eras, which cover the bulk of geologic time, is somewhat sketchy. The first era, Asoic or Cosmic, began with the formation of the earth about 4,500,-000,000 years ago. It ended about 2,000,000,-

An armored fish from the Silurian period

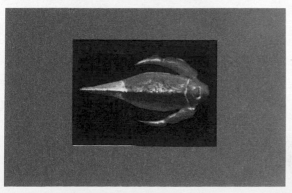

Imprints of ferns on clay rocks from the Pennsylvanian period.

Insects were imprisoned within bits of yellow amber given off by trees.

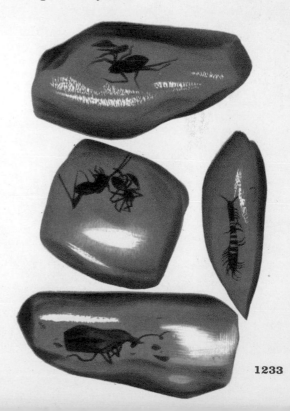

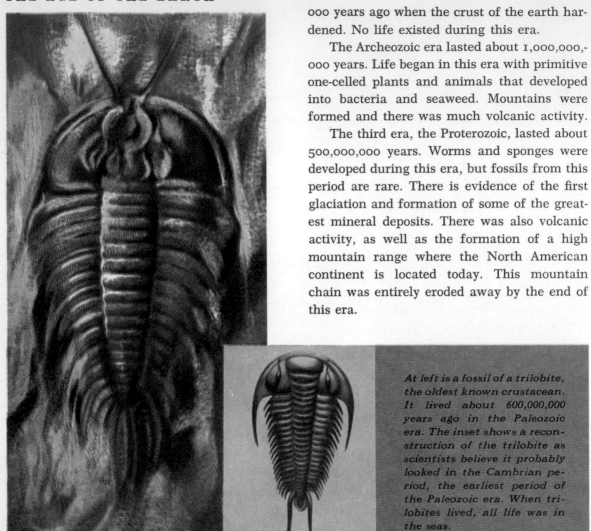

ooo years ago when the crust of the earth hardened. No life existed during this era.

The Archeozoic era lasted about 1,000,000,-ooo years. Life began in this era with primitive one-celled plants and animals that developed into bacteria and seaweed. Mountains were formed and there was much volcanic activity.

The third era, the Proterozoic, lasted about 500,000,000 years. Worms and sponges were developed during this era, but fossils from this period are rare. There is evidence of the first glaciation and formation of some of the greatest mineral deposits. There was also volcanic activity, as well as the formation of a high mountain range where the North American continent is located today. This mountain chain was entirely eroded away by the end of this era.

At left is a fossil of a trilobite, the oldest known crustacean. It lived about 600,000,000 years ago in the Paleozoic era. The inset shows a reconstruction of the trilobite as scientists believe it probably looked in the Cambrian period, the earliest period of the Paleozoic era. When trilobites lived, all life was in the seas.

Imprint of a teleostean fish from the Cenozoic age.

Fossilized tooth of a selachian fish

Times during these first three eras are determined entirely by radioactive decay. During the last three eras, data has been gathered by both radioactivity and stratigraphy.

The fourth, or Paleozoic, era began about 600,000,000 years ago. This era consists of seven periods, given in decreasing order of age —Cambrian, Ordovician, Silurian, Devonian, Mississippian, Pennsylvanian, and Permian. Sometimes all of geologic time preceding the Paleozoic era is referred to as Pre-Cambrian. During this era, many layers of thick sediment, eventually becoming sedimentary rock, were deposited at the bottom of shallow seas that now make up the continents. Some of these layers have been folded or bent by extreme pressure and have formed mountains. There were other mountains formed by volcanic activity. There are indications of glaciation in the Southern Hemisphere. Oil and gas fields were formed in North America. The Pennsylvanian period, known for the vast coal deposits that were formed, was named by geologists for the location in which coal deposits were found.

There are three ages of life during this era —the Age of Trilobites, or boneless marine life, the Age of Fishes, and the Age of Amphibians. There was life only in the sea during the Age of Trilobites. The Age of Fishes saw the first air-breathing animals, which were scorpions, and the first land plants. These land plants developed into the early forests. Dur-

ing the Age of Amphibians, insects and reptiles appeared for the first time, along with the development of the amphibians. Dragonflies and cockroaches reached gigantic size. Forests became widespread, particularly those that, as they died and decayed, left vast carbon deposits in the earth.

The Mesozoic era, sometimes called the Age of Reptiles, is divided into three periods— the Triassic, the Jurassic, and the Cretaceous. It began about 200,000,000 years ago when the Appalachian Mountains were formed. During this era many layers of sedimentary rock that make up the Colorado Plateau were deposited. These are now seen in the Grand Canyon of the Colorado River. Volcanic mountains were also formed, and there was extensive faulting. Faulting is a fracture in the earth's

MAMMALS OF THE CENOZOIC ERA

Many of the mammals of Cenozoic era were similar to their modern descendants. These included the mastodon from which the elephant is descended, the saber-toothed tiger, the eohippus which was the ancestor of today's horse, although tiny and five-toed, and a doglike animal from which not only dogs but bears evolved.

The Brontosaurus, one of the largest dinosaurs, lived during the Jurassic and Cretaceous periods.

crust with movement along the fracture by one or both sides, like in an earthquake. The major plant activity was the spread of cone-bearing trees and the development of flowering plants. The first primitive mammals and birds appeared, and reptiles, including giant dinosaurs, flying dragons, and sea serpents, developed.

The Cenozoic era, which includes the present day, began about 70,000,000 years ago. It consists of two periods—the Tertiary and the Quaternary. These are further divided into seven epochs. The epochs, in order of decreasing age, are Paleocene, Eocene, Oligocene, Miocene, Pliocene, Pleistocene, and Holocene, or Recent. The last two belong to the Quaternary period, which is called the Age of Man. The Tertiary period is called the Age of Mammals. The formation of the great mountain ranges occurred during the Miocene epoch. The Ice Age occurred during the Pleistocene epoch, and its results can still be seen today. The present land forms have been shaped by erosion, the action of streams, waves, wind, and ice.

Plant life similar to the plant life of today evolved about 10,000,000 years ago. At the beginning of the Age of Mammals a small, five-toed horse, about the size of a cat, appeared. Later, small monkeys and elephants developed. They began to look like the present-day monkeys and elephants about 1,000,000 years ago. Man first appeared during the Pleistocene epoch, at a time when mastodons, mammoths, and saber-toothed tigers roamed the earth. During the Holocene, or Recent, epoch, modern civilizations have developed and plants and animals have changed into those we know today.

Recently, using the radioactive method of dating rocks and fossils, scientists have established that man existed on the North American continent 37,000 years ago. Although this is much longer than scientists previously thought, it is almost insignificant in geologic time.

The mammoth (1), *hairy rhinoceros* (2), *and the cave bear* (3) *were the last great mammals that roamed the earth before the Ice Age. Early man* (4) *as he may have appeared during the Pleistocene epoch*

TIME CHART
VOLUME 14

represents all time from the beginning of the earth to the present, which is calculated by most authorities to be four to six billion years. The lowest band covers a period of 1,000 years, counting back from the present to A.D. 1000. The band above it covers 4,000 years, counting back from the year A.D. 1000 to 5,000 years ago. Each band represents about four times as many years as the band directly below it. The third band covers 16,000 years, the one above it 64,000 years, and so on. As you go back in time, dates become more and more uncertain. Dates before recorded history—about 3000 B.C.—are the calculations and expert guesses of archeologists and geologists.

Oceans form and cool enough for first life

The earth formed, p. 1230

4,000,000,000 TO 6,000,000,000 YEARS AGO

One-celled animals and plants

First life on earth, p. 1230

1,000,000,000

3 OR MORE GLACIAL ERAS

Land plants

350,000,000

EACH

Beginning and end of the dinosaurs

Appalachian Mountains formed, p. 1230

LASTING

100,000,000

ABOUT

Age of Mammals

ONE

20,000,000

MILLION

YEARS

5,000,000

Early man makes his first fire and first implements   p. 1164

1,250,000

350,000

LAST
GLACIAL
ERA

Development of Stone Age man

90,000

Cave paintings and pictures carved on bone tools

20,000

Ur, first city, has gold and copper

City of Mohenjo-Daro, India, p. 1224

Egyptian pyramids

5,000 YEARS AGO

= 3000 B.C.

2000 B.C.

1000 B.C.

Height of Greek civilization

Birth of Christ   A.D. 1 B.C.

Height of Roman civilization

A.D. 1000

DARK AGES

1096   First Crusade

Genghis Khan   1206

1300   First gunpowder

Netherlands and Belgium joined to Spain, p. 1156   1460   First printing, first type

RENAISSANCE

Columbus   1492

Treaty of Westphalia, p. 1156   Dutch East India Company, p. 1156
Dutch settlers in South Africa, p. 1198

The Shakespearean Theater, p. 1152

1698   First steam engine

Goya, p. 1186   Cotton gin invented, p. 1193   The Intolerable Acts, p. 1196

Earliest remains of men discovered, p. 1219   The Suez Canal opened, p. 1182

Iraq becomes independent, p. 1208   Radioactivity discovered by Becquerel, p. 1174

Atomic energy   1942

The Suez Canal seized by Nassar, p. 1182   United Arab Republic formed, p. 1208

A.D. 2000

The type in red with page numbers (such as p.1208) refers to Titles and facts in this volume.
Items in black are chosen from the complete chronology in Volume 16 to help place events.

EACH BAND COVERS FOUR TIMES AS MANY YEARS AS THE BAND BELOW IT

16,000 YEARS   4,000 YEARS   1,000 YEARS